HAPPY 60TH BIRTHDAY

FROM

# 1962

# THE NEWS
# THE EVENTS
# AND
# THE LIVES
# OF 1962

ELIZABETH ABSALOM & MALCOLM WATSON

D'AZUR PUBLISHING

First published in Great Britain in 2022 by D'Azur Limited
Contact: info@d-azur.com  Visit www.yearbooks.d-azur.com
ISBN 9798796372241

**ACKNOWLEDGEMENTS**
The publisher wishes to acknowledge the following people and sources:

British Newspaper Archive; The Times Archive;  p4 Queensland State Archives (Queen); history.blog.gov.uk (Harold Macmillan; p20 Free Images; p20 Mathwiz593;  p21: Ben Brooksbank; p23 Unisouth;  p27 UK Defence Journal (UKDJ); p33 The Kali Collective; p35 Fonds André Cros; p37 Sheffield History Forum; p39 Amio Cajander ; p49 Archive Television Musings; p51 Thetillergirls.com p53 Charles01; p59 Andrew Rabbott; p63 Road.org; p79 The Metropolitan Museum of Art. (Cezanne); p85 John Mann Collection;  p89 Tunnel Mont Blanc; p91 Mansfield Chad; p93 The Falkirk Herald; p95 Malcolm Asquith; p99 Toby Hudson; p101 ttypes.org; p103 Library of Congress; p107 Hurawalhi Island Resort;  p117 Donald I. Grant; p119 Eduard Marmet; p123 RAF Museum Cosford; p127 Association for Diplomatic Studies and Training.

Whilst we have made every effort to contact copyright holders, should we have made any omission, please contact us so that we can make the appropriate acknowledgement.

# CONTENTS

# 1962 HIGHLIGHTS

*Monarch - Queen Elizabeth II*

*Prime Minister Harold Macmillan Conservative*

In 1962, Harold Macmillan was presiding over a period of renewed prosperity following the frugality of the immediate post-war years. The country was witnessing the beginnings of a social and cultural revolution, young people were finding a voice and a freedom very different from previous generations, technology was advancing rapidly and the 'consumer society' was taking hold.

It was the era of the Cold War, the threat of nuclear weapons, the Berlin Wall, apartheid in South Africa and the arrest of Nelson Mandela but it was also the dawn of burgeoning activism for civil rights and 'Ban the Bomb'. The 'Space Race' was on, Marilyn Monroe died, the Beatles released 'Love Me Do' and the first 'James Bond' film came out. The 50's 'gramophone' gave way to the 60's 'record player', the contraceptive pill liberated women and the words 'personal computer' were first heard.

Whilst, for older people, fashion in 1962 was still reminiscent of the 50's - conservative and restrained, the young were being influenced by the hair styles and fashion of the emerging popular bands, 'drain pipe' jeans and 'sloppy Joe' jumpers were de rigeur.

*Marilyn Monroe*

## FAMOUS PEOPLE WHO WERE BORN IN 1962

Jan 20th Sophie Thompson, English actress
Feb 7th: Eddie Izzard, British actor
Feb 21st:Vanessa Feltz, British television
Mar 23rd:Sir Steve Redgrave, English rower
May 2nd:Jimmy White, British snooker player
July 3rd:Tom Cruise, American actor
Sept 2nd:Keir Starmer, English politician
Nov 19th:Jodie Foster, American actress
Dec 22nd:Ralph Fiennes, English actor

## FAMOUS PEOPLE WHO DIED IN 1962

Apr 4th:James Hanratty, English murderer
Apr 21st:Sir Frederick Handley Page, English aircraft manufacturer (b.1885)
Jun 1st:Adolph Eichmann, German SS (executed)
Aug 5th:Marilyn Monroe, American actress
Nov 7th:Eleanor Roosevelt, First Lady of the United States (b. 1884)
Dec 15th:Charles Laughton, English actor and director (b.1899)

## THE YEAR'S HEADLINES

**JANUARY**   Pope John XXIII excommunicates Fidel Castro, revolutionary and President of Cuba.
US Air Force sprays South Vietnamese forests with defoliants.

**FEBRUARY**   John Glenn becomes the first American to orbit the Earth.
The US embargo against Cuba is announced.

**MARCH**   France and Algeria sign an agreement in Évians les Bains, ending the Algerian War.

**APRIL**   The American Ranger 4 spacecraft crashes into the Moon.
Georges Pompidou becomes Prime Minister of France.

**MAY**   The new Coventry Cathedral is consecrated in England.
Nazi war criminal Adolf Eichmann is hanged at a prison in Israel.

**JUNE**   The last soldiers of the French Foreign Legion leave Algeria.

**JULY**   Charles de Gaulle accepts Algerian independence.
In "the Night of the Long Knives", Harold Macmillan dismisses one-third of his Cabinet.

**AUGUST**   Nelson Mandela is arrested by the South African government and charged with incitement to rebellion.
Jamaica and Trinidad & Tobago both become independent from Britain.

**SEPTEMBER**   The United Nations announces that the Earth's population has hit 3 billion.
The Soviet Union agrees to send arms to Cuba.

**OCTOBER**   The Cuban Missile Crisis brings the world to the brink of a world war.

**NOVEMBER**   The Cuban blockade ends.

**DECEMBER**   Britain agrees to purchase Polaris missiles from the U.S.
Cuba releases the last 1,113 U.S. Troops captured in the "Bay of Pigs Invasion" in exchange for food worth $53 million.

## FILMS AND ARTS

**FILMS**  The 34th Academy Awards Ceremony is held. **"West Side Story"** wins Best Picture.

16th Tony Awards: **"A Man For All Seasons"** & **"How to Succeed in Business Without Really Trying"** win.

New Films released include: **"Lolita"** starring James Mason and Sue Lyon. **"Dr No"**, the first James Bond film, starring Sean Connery and Ursula Andress.

**"What Ever Happened to Baby Jane?"** a horror film with Bette Davis and **"Lawrence of Arabia"** starring Peter O'Toole, Omar Sharif, Alec Guinness, Jack Hawkins and Anthony Quinn.

**ARTS  Margot Fonteyn and Rudolf Nureyev** first dance together in a Royal Ballet performance of Giselle, in London.

American artist **Andy Warhol** premieres his "Campbell's Soup Cans" exhibit in Los Angeles.

John Steinbeck, American author is awarded the Nobel Prize in Literature. Aleksandr Solzhenitsyn's novella, **"One Day in the Life of Ivan Denisovich"** is published in Russia.

The first episode of **"That Was the Week that Was"**, the ground-breaking satirical comedy program is broadcast on BBC Television.

# 1962 THE YEAR

*These terraced houses in London had no back gardens so washing was hung from one side of the street to another. Holidays may have been a day trip to the Kent coast.*

*Football Pools were a 'betting pool' for predicting the outcome of top-level football matches taking place in the coming week. It was typically cheap to play and entries were sent to Littlewoods or Vernons, by post, or collected from your home by agents.*

*The most popular game was the Treble Chance where you had to predict the matches to end in a 'draw'.*

Despite being seventeen years after the end of WWII, 1962 saw little prosperity for most people in Britain. For many there was one week's paid holiday which was often spent at a British coastal resort.

Few had cars and so were reliant on getting to their holiday destination by train or coach. Within 10 years all of this would have changed.

## MOST POPULAR BABY NAMES

| Rank | Male name | Female name |
|------|-----------|-------------|
| 1 | David | Susan |
| 2 | John | Linda |
| 3 | Stephen | Christine |
| 4 | Michael | Margaret |
| 5 | Peter | Janet |
| 6 | Robert | Patricia |
| 7 | Paul | Carol |
| 8 | Alan | Elizabeth |
| 9 | Christopher | Mary |
| 10 | Richard | Anne |

## HOW MUCH DID IT COST?

| | | |
|---|---|---|
| The Average Pay: | £799 | (£15 p.w) |
| The Average House: | £2,670 | |
| Loaf of White Bread: | 11½ d | (4½p) |
| Pint of Milk: | 8d | (3p) |
| Pint of Beer: | 2s | (10p) |
| Dozen Eggs: | 4s | (20p) |
| Gallon of Petrol: | 4s 8d | (23p) |
| Newspapers: | 2½ d | (1p) |
| To post a letter in UK: | 3d | (1½p) |
| Average Television | £70 (Black and White) | |

*The revolutionary Mini was the fastest selling small car in Britain. It was driven by stars of music and fashion as well as by families on a budget. Despite the promise of the adverts early models were slow and unreliable.*

*Adverts promoted it as a luxury family car but in reality, it was uncomfortable and cramped.*

## POPULAR MUSIC

The top-selling single in the UK in 1962 was the yodelling Frank Ifield's "I Remember You". Cliff Richard was the star of British pop, with "The Young Ones" and "The Next Time/Bachelor Boy" both topping the charts

Chubby Checker's song "The Twist", credited with starting the Twist dance craze, goes to number 1 in the charts two years after first reaching the number one spot.

**March:** "Un premier amour", sung by Isabelle Aubret wins the Eurovision Song Contest for France.

Bob Dylan's debut album "Bob Dylan"is released in the United States.

**May:** Acker Bilk's "Stranger on the Shore" becomes the first British recording to reach number one, in the US Billboard Hot 100.

**July:** The Rolling Stones make their debut at London's Marquee Club, opening for Long John Baldry.

**August:** Ringo Starr replaces Pete Best as the Beatles' drummer.

Peter, Paul & Mary release their first hit "If I Had a Hammer"

**October:** The Beatles' first single "Love Me Do"/ "P.S. I Love You", is released in the U.K. but only managed No 17 in the charts.

Brian Epstein signs a contract to manage The Beatles until 1977.

American singer Barbra Streisand signs her 1st recording contract with Columbia.

**December:** "Telstar" by The Tornados becomes the first single by a British group to reach No. 1 on the US charts, predating The Beatles by 13 months.

By 1967, Carnaby Street was popular with followers of the mod and hippie styles. Many fashion designers, such as Mary Quant, Lord John and Irvine Sellars, had premises in the street and underground music bars, such as the Roaring Twenties, opened in the surrounding streets. Bands such as the Small Faces, The Who and The Rolling Stones appeared in the area, to work (at the legendary Marquee Club round the corner in Wardour Street), to shop, and to socialise. The Street became one of the coolest destinations associated with 1960s Swinging London.

*The late 1960s saw a massive change in fashion.*

*Dresses, suits. Ties and hats were being spurned by the young who wanted flamboyant and striking clothes. The mini skirt became the fashion statement for young women.*

## MOST POPULAR BABY NAMES

| Rank | Male name | Female name |
|------|-----------|-------------|
| 1 | David | Susan |
| 2 | Paul | Julie |
| 3 | Andrew | Karen |
| 4 | Mark | Jacqueline |
| 5 | John | Deborah |
| 6 | Michael | Tracey |
| 7 | Stephen | Jane |
| 8 | Ian | Helen |
| 9 | Robert | Diane |
| 10 | Richard | Sharon |

## HOW MUCH DID IT COST?

| | | |
|---|---|---|
| The Average Pay: | £890 | (£17 p.w) |
| The Average House: | £3,735 | |
| Loaf of White Bread: | 1s 2d | (6p) |
| Pint of Milk: | 10d | (4p) |
| Pint of Beer: | 2s 6d | (12.5p) |
| Dozen Eggs: | 4d | (20p) |
| Gallon of Petrol: | 4s 7d | (23p) |
| Newspapers: | 4d | (1.5p) |
| To post a letter in UK: | 4d | (1.5p) |
| Average Television | £279 (Colour) | |

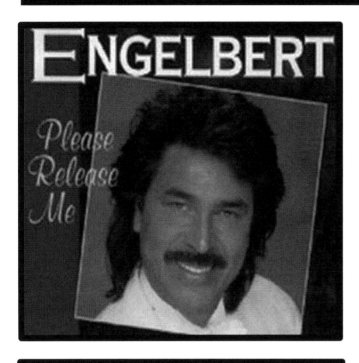

**How to make Dad's day.**

"Quick Brew is the third largest selling brand in both the Tea Bag and Packet Tea markets in the United Kingdom." *

*Lyons Tetley*

*It was Tetley in 1953 that drove the introduction of tea bags in Britain, but other companies soon caught up. In the early 1960s, tea bags made up less than 3 per cent of the British market, but this has been growing steadily ever since. The key selling points were no tea leaves to dispose of and the fact that a tea pot was not needed - you could make the tea directly in the cup.*

## POPULAR MUSIC

1967 Was the "Year of Love" in San Francisco.

Engelbert Humperdinck had the best-selling single of the year, the six-week chart-topper "Release Me". He also had the second and last UK number-one single of his career, the five-week chart-topper "The Last Waltz".

**March:** On tour with The Walker Brothers, Cat Stevens and Engelbert Humperdinck at The Astoria London, Jimi Hendrix sets fire to his guitar on stage for the first time. He is taken to hospital suffering burns to his hands. The guitar-burning act would later become a trademark of Hendrix's performances.

**April:** The 12th Eurovision Song Contest is won by Britain for the first time with "Puppet on a String", sung by Sandie Shaw.

**May:** Procol Harum release their debut single, "A Whiter Shade of Pale". It reached number 1 in the UK Singles Chart on 8 June and stayed there for six weeks

**June:** The Beatles released "Sgt. Pepper's Lonely Hearts Club Band", one of rock's most acclaimed albums.
Barbra Streisand performs a live concert "A Happening in Central Park" in New York's Central Park before 135,000 people.

**September:** Tony Blackburn launches the new BBC Radio 1 by playing "Flowers in the Rain" by The Move.

"All My Love" by Cliff Richard, "Daydream Believer" by The Monkees, Magical Mystery Tour" by The Beatles and "Thank U Very Much" by The Scaffold were all released in 1967 but did not reach their peak until 1968

The traditional cafe was losing business to the new 'fast food' outlets such as KFC and MacDonald's. Slow ordering and service with food served at tables was not as attractive as the fast service, clean and lower cost experience of the USA brands. Eating became fun and fried finger food was very attractive to children.

*Eating with cutlery on a plate with tea in a mug served by staff meant that traditional cafes had higher overheads than fast food outlets who used disposable plates and cups and with no waiting staff had lower costs and lower prices.*

## MOST POPULAR BABY NAMES

| Rank | Male name | Female name |
|------|-----------|-------------|
| 1 | Paul | Sarah |
| 2 | Mark | Claire |
| 3 | David | Nicola |
| 4 | Andrew | Emma |
| 5 | Richard | Lisa |
| 6 | Christopher | Joanne |
| 7 | James | Michelle |
| 8 | Simon | Helen |
| 9 | Michael | Samantha |
| 10 | Matthew | Karen |

## HOW MUCH DID IT COST?

| | |
|---|---|
| The Average Pay: | £2,236  (£43 p.w) |
| The Average House: | £9,045 |
| Loaf of White Bread: | 11p |
| Pint of Milk: | 6p |
| Pint of Beer: | 18p |
| Dozen Eggs: | 33p |
| Gallon of Petrol: | 38p |
| Newspapers: | 4p |
| To post a letter in UK: | 3.5p |
| Average Television | £209 (Colour) |

*Popular TV programmes included: Last of the Summer Wine, Kojak, Some Mothers Do 'Ave 'Em, Whatever Happened To the Likely Lads?, and That's Life! The main soaps were Emmerdale (started 1972) and Coronation Street (1960). Radio's The Archers had started in 1951.*

## POPULAR MUSIC

Dawn featuring Tony Orlando had the best-selling single of 1973 with "Tie a Yellow Ribbon Round the 'Ole Oak Tree", which spent four weeks at the top spot and lasted 11 weeks in the top 10.

The 1972 Christmas number 1, "Long Haired Lover from Liverpool", by Little Jimmy Osmond remained at number-one for the first three weeks of 1973. The first new number-one single of the year was "Blockbuster" by The Sweet.

**March:** Pink Floyd releases "The Dark Side of the Moon" which goes on to become one of the best-selling albums of all time.

**April:** Cliff Richard finishes in 3rd place in the Eurovision Song Contest with "Power to all Our Friends".

**May:** Mike Oldfield's "Tubular Bells" becomes the first release on Richard Branson's newly launched Virgin label.

**July:** Queen release their debut album, "Queen". The Carpenters reach number 2 with "Yesterday Once More".

**September:** "For the Good Times" by Perry Como stays at number 1 for three weeks.

**October:** Elton John tops the charts with "Goodbye Yellow Brick Road".

David Bowie peaked in the top 10 with five singles in 1973. He reached number two in January with "The Jean Genie", while "Drive in Saturday"(April), "Life on Mars " (June) and "Sorrow" (October) all peaked at number three. His single "The Laughing Gnome", also reached number six in October.

Most housework was very time consuming. Meals were prepared from scratch, ready meals being rare and poor. Washing up was done by hand and laundry had only just moved to machines.

Twin tubs (one for washing and one for spinning) became popular in the late 1960s and were usually wheeled into the kitchen to be attached to the cold tap and have the waste water empty into the sink. Some machines had the ability to pump used wash water into a separate tub for temporary storage, and to later pump it back for re-use. This was done not to save water or soap, but because heated water was expensive and time-consuming to produce. The operator had, however, to be available to move the wet washing from the washing tub to the spinning tub.

Automatic washing machines did not become dominant in the UK until well into the 1970s and by then were almost exclusively of the front-loader design. They could therefore be fitted under worktops and plumbed in saving time and space.

They could also be be switched on and left running without supervision whilst the household were out. This, together with other labour saving devices, meant that more and more women went out to work.

## MOST POPULAR BABY NAMES

| Rank | Male name | Female name |
|------|-----------|-------------|
| 1 | David | Sarah |
| 2 | Christopher | Claire |
| 3 | James | Samantha |
| 4 | Paul | Emma |
| 5 | Andrew | Amy |
| 6 | Michael | Laura |
| 7 | Mark | Rachelle |
| 8 | Richard | Victoria |
| 9 | Matthew | Rebecca |
| 10 | Simon | Gemma |

## HOW MUCH DID IT COST?

| | |
|---|---|
| The Average Pay: | £5,250  (£101 p.w) |
| The Average House: | £19,830 |
| Loaf of White Bread: | 29p |
| Pint of Milk: | 15p |
| Pint of Beer: | 34p |
| Dozen Eggs: | 55p |
| Gallon of Petrol: | 88p |
| Newspapers: | 8p |
| To post a letter in UK: | 10p |
| Average Television | £260 (Colour) |

## POPULAR MUSIC

Spending five weeks at the top of the British charts in the spring, Boney M's "Rivers of Babylon" became the biggest selling single of the year, exceeding one million sales between May and June.

The Bee Gees' "Saturday Night Fever" becomes the biggest-selling album of all time.

**January:** "Mull of Kintyre" by Wings made number 1 for its ninth and final week - becoming the biggest-selling single in UK history at that point.

**March:** Kate Bush became the first female solo artist to reach number one in the UK charts with a self-written song, "Wuthering Heights".

**April and May:** "Night Fever" from the film, Saturday Night Fever, put the Bee Gees at number 1.

**May:** "The Buddy Holly Story" is released and later wins the Academy Award for Best Music and Original Song Score.

**June, July and August:** From the film Grease, "You're the One That I Want" and "Summer Nights" in September and October, locked up the number 1 position for a total of sixteen weeks. John Travolta and Olivia Newton-John seemed to be constantly in the public conscience.

**September:** The Who drummer Keith Moon died after a prescription drug overdose at the age of 32.

**December:** Rod Stewart was number 1 with "Do Ya Think I'm Sexy?" before Boney M won the Christmas top spot with "Mary's Boy Child – Oh My Lord."

*Package tours to sunny, warm and cheap holiday destinations were very popular by 1978. Companies such as Thompson, Horizon, Global and Clarksons all used chartered planes to fly families to booming resorts where new hotel rooms were being built and offered at low prices.*

*Once there, holiday makers found that in addition to the sun and sand, food and drink was much cheaper than in the UK and this led to the rapid decline in UK seaside resorts and boom in once sleepy fishing villages such as Benidorm.*

1983 saw a revolution in computing. Previously, business computers had been room sized devices only affordable by large organisations. Then came some simple games machines but in January 1983 The Apple Lisa was launched for US$9,995 (equivalent to $25,970 [£17,000] in 2020) with a five-megabyte hard drive.

A revised model at half the price was launched a year later, but only 10,000 were sold. Then when in 1984 the $2,500 Apple Macintosh was launched, Apple computers really took off.

In 2020, Apple sold 22.5 Million Macbooks at an average price of £1000.

Here is a brief history of computers: 1941: Atanasoff and his graduate student, Clifford Berry, design the first digital electronic computer in the USA capable of performing one operation every 15 seconds.

1975: The magazine "Popular Electronics" highlights the Altair 8080 as the "world's first minicomputer kit to rival commercial models." After seeing the magazine issue, two "computer geeks," Paul Allen and Bill Gates, offer to write software for the Altair, using the new BASIC language. On April 4, after the success of this first endeavour, the two childhood friends form their own software company, Microsoft.

In 1985, Microsoft released a new operating system, Windows, with a graphical user interface that included drop-down menus, scroll bars and other features.

Commodore sold 1 million of these basic home computers between 1980 and 1984. They became the leading game computer of the time whereas Apple was for business and computing enthusiasts. The $399 (£275) price was a fraction of that of an Apple Lisa.

## MOST POPULAR BABY NAMES

| Rank | Male name | Female name |
|---|---|---|
| 1 | Christopher | Sarah |
| 2 | James | Laura |
| 3 | David | Gemma |
| 4 | Daniel | Emma |
| 5 | Michael | Rebecca |
| 6 | Matthew | Claire |
| 7 | Andrew | Victoria |
| 8 | Richard | Semantha |
| 9 | Paul | Rachel |
| 10 | Mark | Amy |

## HOW MUCH DID IT COST?

| | |
|---|---|
| The Average Pay: | £8,320 (£160 p.w) |
| The Average House: | £27,360 |
| Loaf of White Bread: | 38p |
| Pint of Milk: | 21p |
| Pint of Beer: | 70p |
| Dozen Eggs: | 60p |
| Gallon of Petrol: | £2.00 |
| Newspapers: | 16p |
| To post a letter in UK: | 16p |
| Average Television | £320 (Colour) |

CULTURE CLUB
Karma Chameleon

## STAR WARS:
## RETURN OF THE JEDI 1983

*Star Wars: Episode VI – Return of the Jedi) was released on May 25, 1983, receiving positive reviews, although many felt that it did not match the cinematic heights of its predecessors. It grossed £305 million during its initial theatrical run, becoming the highest-grossing film of 1983.*

## POPULAR MUSIC

The UK's best-selling single of 1983 was Culture Club's "Karma Chameleon" with six weeks at number 1 and another four still in the top 10 from September onwards.

**January:** The UK Singles Chart is tabulated from this week forward by The Gallup Organisation, and by 1984 electronic terminals are used in selected stores to gather sales information, the old "sales diary" method being gradually phased out.

The first new number 1 single of the year was "You Can't Hurry Love" by Phil Collins of Genesis.

**February:** Karen Carpenter died at age 32 from heart failure due to complications from anorexia nervosa.

**March:** Bonnie Tyler claims the year's best-selling track by a female artist, and is the only woman in the Top 10, with "Total Eclipse of the Heart". Her first and only number 1 single spent two weeks at the top.

**April:** David Bowie releases "Let's Dance". Produced by Nile Rodgers, with a deliberate shift to mainstream dance-rock, it became his biggest commercial success with 10.7 million copies sold worldwide.

**August:** The Rolling Stones sign a new $28 million contract with CBS Records, the largest recording contract in history up to this time.

**September:** UB40, the reggae-pop band, logged three weeks at number 1 with "Red Red Wine".

**November and December:** Billy Joel's global hit "Uptown Girl" stays top for five weeks.

## SPORTING HEADLINES

**Mar: The Grand National** was won by Fred Winter on "Kilmore", a 28/1 shot.

Fred Winter was also the winning jockey in The **Cheltenham Gold Cup**, riding "Mandarin".

**Apr:** Tottenham Hotspur win the **FA Cup Final** beating Burnley 3-1 at Wembley.

In the **Rugby Five Nations** (now Six Nations) Championship, France were the winners.

The **Rugby County Championship** was won by Warwickshire who beat Hampshire 11-6

Rangers beat St Mirren 2-1 in the **Scottish Cup Final** at Hampden Park.

26th **US Masters Golf Tournament**, Augusta. Arnold Palmer wins the 3rd of his 4 Masters titles.

**May:** In the **European Cup Final** in Amsterdam, Benfica (Portugal) beat Real Madrid (Spain), 5-3.

**June:** Brazil beats Czechoslovakia 3-1 to win the **1962 FIFA World Cup**.

Jack Nicklaus wins his first major title at the **US Open** Men's Golf,

Larkspur wins **The Derby** in a race marred by mayhem when seven horses fell.

**July** At **Wimbledon** in the Men's Tennis Final, Rod Laver beat fellow Australian, Martin Mulligan.
In the Women's Tennis Final, American Karen Susman beat Vera Suková of Czechoslovakia.

At **The Open** golf tournament, played at Royal Troon, Arnold Palmer won for the second time.

*The 1962 FA Cup Winners Tottenham Hotspur*

**Jul:** The 49th **Tour de France** was won by defending champion Jacques Anquetil of France. His third win.

**Sept:** Sonny Liston knocked out Floyd Pattison after two minutes into the first round of the **Boxing World Title** fight in Chicago.

In sailing, the **1962 America's Cup** was won by the New York Yacht Club's boat Weatherly.

Yorkshire won the **Cricket County Championship**

**The St Leger**, run at Doncaster, was won by Hethersett ridden by Harry Carr.

**Oct:** The **Scottish League Cup Final** was contested by Kilmarnock and Heart of Midlothian. Hearts won the match 1–0.

**Nov: The Commonwealth Games** began in Perth, Australia.

**Dec:** British driver Graham Hill wins the **South African Grand Prix** in a BRM. This wins his first **F1 World Drivers Championship** by 12 points from Scotsman Jim Clark.

*The 1962 Formula One Season was won by Graham Hill (see inset photo) driving a BRM car*

## THE 1962 FORMULA ONE SEASON

The 1962 Formula One season featured the World Championship of Drivers and the International Cup for F1 Manufacturers, which were contested simultaneously over nine races that started on 20 May and ended on 29 December. This was the first year of the South African Grand Prix which meant the Championship would be held in three continents.

Phil Hill and his Ferrari were the defending Champions, but Ferrari was to be completely eclipsed this season by the British teams, BRM and Lotus.

The first four races saw three first time winners, Graham Hill in his BRM in the Netherlands, Jim Clark in his monocoque Lotus 25 at Belgium and American Dan Gurney, winning in a Porsche in France.

The rest of the season's wins were shared between Jim Clark and Graham Hill, with Clark dominating the British Grand Prix. When they reached the South African Grand Prix, the last of the season, they had three wins each, but with Hill holding a nine-point lead over Clark. Jim Clark took pole position as they went 'head to head' for the title. He made an excellent start staying ahead of Hill until with 20 laps to go the Lotus began to trail blue smoke and on lap 63 of 82, the Scot was out with an oil leak. Graham Hill, for his part, finished the race without mishap to win his fourth race of the season and his first World Championship title.

### "West Side Story" Wins The Academy Awards "Best Picture" category.

The musical with lyrics by Stephen Sondheim and music by Leonard Bernstein was inspired by the story of William Shakespeare's "Romeo and Juliet". Set in the mid 1950s in Upper West Side of New York City, which was then, a cosmopolitan working-class area, it follows the rivalry between the Jets and the Sharks, two teenage street gangs from different ethnic backgrounds.

The Sharks are from Puerto Rico and are taunted by the white Jets gang. The hero, Tony, a former member of the Jets falls in love with Maria, the sister of the leader of the Sharks. The sophisticated music and the extended dance scenes, focussing on the social problems marked a turning point in musical theatre. The film starred Natalie Wood and Richard Beymer.

### Dr No", The First James Bond Film, In London."

This was the first-ever launch of a James Bond film in a cinema and was attended by the stars, Sean Connery and Ursula Andress together with the James Bond creator Ian Fleming. This British spy film, adapted from the 1958 novel written by Ian Fleming, was filmed in Jamaica and England and produced by Harry Saltzman and Albert R. Broccoli.

The plot revolves around James Bond who needs to solve the mystery of the strange disappearance of a British agent to Jamaica and finds an underground base belonging to Dr No who is plotting to disrupt the American space launch with a radio beam weapon. The film was condemned by The Vatican as "a dangerous mixture of violence, vulgarity, sadism, and sex".

**"American Artist Andy Warhol premieres his "Campbell's Soup Cans" Exhibit In Los Angeles".**

Andy Warhol famously borrowed familiar icons from everyday life and the media, among them celebrity and tabloid news photos, comic strips, and, in this work, the popular canned soup made by the Campbell's Soup Company.

When he first exhibited "Campbell's Soup Cans", the images were displayed together on shelves, like products in a grocery aisle. At the time, Campbell's sold 32 soup varieties and each one of Warhol's 32 canvasses corresponds to a different flavour, each having a different label. The first flavour, introduced in 1897, was tomato.

Each canvas was hand painted and the fleur de lys pattern round each can's bottom edge was hand stamped. Warhol said, "I used to drink Campbell's Soup. I used to have the same lunch every day, for 20 years, I guess!"

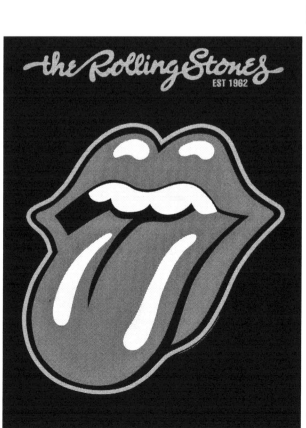

**"The Rolling Stones Make Their Debut At London's Marquee Club".**

"Blues Incorporated", Alexis Korner's band had a regular Thursday night gig at the Marquee Club in London's Oxford Street. In the first week of July, Korner was invited on to BBC Radio's Jazz Club and asked his friends Mick Jagger, Ian Stewart, Keith Richards and Brian Jones to deputize for him at the Marquee. Jones intended for the band to play primary Chicago Blues but Jagger and Richards decided to play the rock 'n roll of Chuck Berry and Bo Diddley.

Bassist Bill Wyman joined in December and drummer Charlie Watts the following January to form the long-standing Stones rhythm section.
The Band embarked on their first UK tour in July 1963 and played their first gig outside greater London at the Outlook Club in Middlesbrough for which they were paid £40. They shared the billing that night with the Hollies.

### Total Eclipse of the Sun

In February there was an extremely rare "great conjunction" of the Moon, Mercury, Venus, the Sun, Mars, Jupiter and Saturn. This was the first occurrence since 1821 and all the "classical planets" were within 16° of one another with Saturn, Jupiter, Mars and Venus on one side of the Sun and Mercury and Earth on the opposite.

At the same time there was a total eclipse of the Sun, which was visible in Asia, Australia and the Pacific Ocean. A total eclipse is when the Moon passes between the Earth and the Sun and the Moon's "apparent diameter" is larger than the Sun's thereby blocking all sunlight and turning day into darkness. In India, anticipation of the events had led to wide-spread predictions of the 'end of the world' to begin.

Write-Protect Tab    Supply Reel    Slip Sheet    Take-up Reel

Guide Roller    Magnetic Shield    Pressure Pad    Capstan Hole

### Cassette Tape

Although the cassette tape was not released to the world until the following year, it was first developed by Philips in Belgium in 1962. These two small spools inside its plastic case, which wind magnetic-coated film and pass it from one side to the other, meant music could now be recorded and shared by everyone.

Not only could you record your favourite songs, but you could create your own mixed tapes and not just for yourself. Taking the time to compile and record selected tracks showed true devotion for a friend or sweetheart! However, the original purpose of the compact cassette tape was for dictation, but it was the passion to use it for music that led to more than 3 billion tapes being sold over its lifetime from 1962 until 1988.

### The Last London Trolleybus

Trolleybuses were taken out of service in London in May having served since 1931. The largest trolleybus system in the world, it peaked at 68 routes with a maximum fleet of 1,811.

Before trolleybuses, trams had taken over public transport from the horse drawn bus which had needed eleven horses to run a 60 miles per day service. Trams were clean, efficient and even glamorous but installing the tracks exactly where they needed to be proved problematical.

A trolleybus drew power from dual overhead cables suspended from roadside posts using spring-loaded 'trolley poles' and were double deckers, 30ft long and crucially, they were much quieter.

However, by the end of the 50's more flexibility was required on routes, one way systems were beginning to appear, traffic congestion itself increased and trolleybuses gave way to motor buses.

### Science, Technology and Nature

**Jan:** Landslides on Mount Huascaran in Peru kill over 4,000.

**May:** US performs atmospheric nuclear test at Christmas Island.

**July:** A heavy smog develops over London.

**Nov:** Earliest recorded use of the term "personal computer" in the report of a speech by computing pioneer John Mauchley in The New York Times.

An agreement is signed between Britain and France, to develop the "Concorde" supersonic airliner.

**Dec:** In the UK, the "Big Freeze" begins. There are no frost-free nights until March 5th, 1963.

### London Smog

This December, London suffered under a choking blanket of smog, redolent of the Great Smog of 1952 when as many as 12,000 people had died. Since then, the 'Clean Air Act' which introduced smokeless zones in urban areas had been introduced but it was taking time for people to change habits and stop burning domestic fuels such as coal. Smog is a concentration of smoke particles and other substances such as sulphur dioxide, combined with fog in conditions of low temperature, high pressure and lack of wind. Visibility was reduced such that a light could only be seen at 50ft and in spite of people covering their faces with scarves, surgical masks or handkerchieves the overwhelming smell of sulphur and coal smoke left an unpleasant metallic taste in the mouth and irritated eyes and noses. Bronchitis increased significantly and it is estimated that, in Greater London alone, there were 700 deaths in total.

Born in 1962, you were one of 53 million people living in Britain and your life expectancy *then* was 71 years. You were one of the 17 births per 1,000 population and you had a 2.2% chance of dying as an infant, most likely from an infectious disease such as polio, diphtheria, tetanus, whooping cough, measles, mumps or rubella.

You could "Listen with Mother" on the wireless and if you were in one of the 74% of households who owned a television set, with only two channels BBC and ITV to choose from, you might have watched: "Bill and Ben The Flower Pot Men", "Andy Pandy", "Sooty" and "It's Friday, it's Five to Five and it's Crackerjack".

Your parents might have watched these new shows: "Z Cars", "Steptoe and Son", "Police Five", "University Challenge" and "That Was the Week That Was."

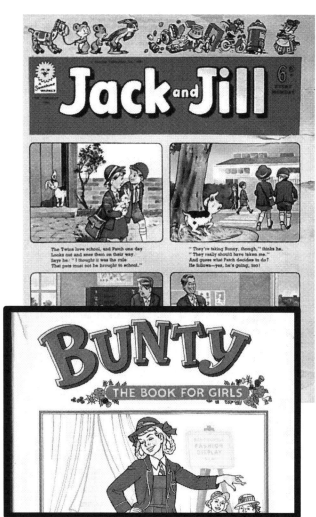

Your pocket money, probably 6d (2.5p) a week, would buy sweets. Black Jacks and Fruit Salads (4 for a penny (0.5p)), sweet cigarettes, lemonade crystals, gob stoppers, flying saucers or toffees, weighed by the shopkeeper in 2oz or 4oz paper bags. All to be eaten whilst reading your Beano or Dandy, Bunty or Jack and Jill comics.

In 1962 the nuclear family was the norm, father out at work and mother busy with the housework which was labour intensive before the general possession of washing machines and hoovers, electric irons and tumble dryers.

Only 33% of households had a refrigerator, so shopping was done daily and, typically, all meals were home cooked.

Chicken was expensive but beef was cheaper and olive oil came only in tiny bottles from the chemist to help clean your ears!

## BUTLIN'S HOLIDAY CAMP SKEGNESS

At eleven you sat the 11+ exam and went to grammar school or secondary modern. At home you might have had a set of Encyclopaedia Britannica to help with your homework, sold door to door on "easy terms".

Your holiday during the 6 week summer break was likely to be in Britain. Holiday camps such as Butlins with their 'Red Coats' offered hours of fun, coaches could take you to the seaside and owning a caravan was becoming popular too. If you ate out, fish and chips was the most usual but Chinese restaurants were on the increase and teenagers loved the 'Wimpy Bar' for burgers. Born in 1962 you were at the beginning of the age where young people were finally given a voice and freedom to do what they wanted.

Goods came to you. The milkman delivered the milk to your doorstep, the baker brought the baskets of bread to the door, the greengrocer delivered and the 'pop man' came once a week with 'dandelion and burdock', 'cherryade' or 'cream soda' and the rag and bone man visited the street for your recycling.

# JANUARY 1ST - 7TH 1962

## IN THE NEWS

**Monday 1**    "**Freezing Britain slithers to a halt**". Snow and ice bring chaos to transport. Villages cut off, vehicles abandoned, buses and trains stopped.

**Tuesday 2**    "**Big Car Firms Moving into Contract Hire Field**". Rising Demand from Industry. News of the Ford Motor Company's entry into the contract hire business brought speculation on whether other manufacturers will soon be launching similar schemes.

**Wednesday 3**    "**Post Office deny priority for Football Pools Coupons**". The Post Office said that Pools Coupons always got special treatment because of the large volume, but not preferential or priority treatment over the "fully paid public posted correspondence".

**Thursday 4**    "**A Thaw and it's so Sudden**" bringing an end to the big freeze in London and the southeast last night. However, it brought another hazard, thick fog and then drizzle which washed away the fog and the slush.

**Friday 5**    "**Shoe King Charles Clore in £28m Golden Slipper bid**" Clore is to take over Saxone and acquire a further 475 shops, bringing his total to around 2,000, more than half the retail shoe trade.

**Saturday 6**    "**Big Take Over Battle After 'NO' to ICI**". Directors of Courtaulds, the giant textile firm, last night turned down the £180m take-over offer from Imperial Chemical Industries. Now the stage seems set for the biggest take-over battle Britain has ever seen.

**Sunday 7**    "**Just Like Bruce but Not Quite**". Norman Vaughan took over as host of ITV's "Sunday Night at the London Palladium" but was working under a 'great handicap'. He looked too much like the previous host Bruce Forsyth. "It was inevitable to compare him with the 'Fabulous Mr F—-' and he fell far short of the original"!

## HERE IN BRITAIN

### "Baby Nearly Freezes To Death"

Happy and lively, a baby romped in a childrens' home whilst police searched for her parents.

On New Year's Eve life turned bleak for the baby … she was dumped in the snow outside a hospital in Tamworth and a passer-by found her crawling along the pavement in the icy and slushy snow.

The nurses have named her Mary.

## AROUND THE WORLD

A Broadway producer sent a full-page review to seven New York City newspapers with the headline **"7 OUT OF 7 ARE ECSTATICALLY UNANIMOUS ABOUT 'SUBWAYS ARE FOR SLEEPING'"**, his musical comedy that had opened to poor reviews.

This review contained favourable quotes, from seven friends, men with the same names as real critics. The New York Herald-Tribune ran the advert before an editor spotted the hoax and alerted the other newspapers.

# SNOWED IN!

Chaos arrived when most of Britain was covered by a blanket of snow which froze hard as the temperature dropped.

Villages were cut off, buses and cars stranded and rail services badly hit. The AA reported that every county was affected by ice or snow, except Cornwall, the eastern part of Norfolk and Suffolk, and parts of Lincolnshire.

A widow living near Huddersfield had lain helpless with a broken leg in deep snow for more than seven hours but was rescued alive because of the devotion of Sandy, a neighbour's golden retriever. The dog snuggled up close to the woman and the warmth saved her from freezing to death and, by licking her face, stopped her from falling into a sleep from which she would never have recovered.

Flights were halted when London Airport was shut for fifteen hours, the worst disruption since 1948. In contrast, the flower growers in the Scilly Isles were busy picking outdoor grown daffodils. The temperature there fell to only 43° F (6° C).

When the thaw came it came so quickly that it surprised the weathermen and brought thick fog, reducing visibility to ten yards in certain parts of Kent and Essex and twenty yards in the Midlands and East Anglia. For thousands of householders the onset of the thaw brought fresh hardships and discomfort - water wastage and shortages resulted from burst pipes.

## IN THE NEWS

**Monday 8**    "**Now Miners Will Get a Pay Offer**". Miners are to be offered a wage increase. It is not likely to satisfy their union leaders, but it is one sign that the Government is moving away from the present total "freeze" on pay in the nationalised industries.

**Tuesday 9**    "**Car Body Firm Orders Piling Up.**" ."The rising demand for cars and the resulting increase output of models in Britain's car factories means that The Pressed Steel Company has offered back jobs to 500 workers made redundant 14 months ago.

**Wednesday 10**    "**Adenauer: We'll Pay**". Macmillan wins help for Britain. Germany realised the extreme gravity of the British balance of payments problem and they are just as unwilling to adopt solutions such as any reduction in the strength of the Rhine Army.

**Thursday 11**    "**Parcel-Post Bombshell Hits Britain**". In a shock move yesterday to attempt to break the Post Office work-to-rule pay protest, no parcels could be posted in London for delivery in other parts of Britain and no parcels could be posted from the provinces TO London.

**Friday 12**    "**A Trail of Gale Damage**". Four killed by falling trees and crew picked up after ship sinks. The gales caused heavy damage to property and shipping and serious disruption to transport. A passenger bridge at New Brighton Pier crashed into the river Mersey.

**Saturday 13**    "**Smallpox Alert in Two Towns**". The fight against smallpox intensified yesterday after two deaths in Bradford and five children were isolated. The US Government "closed borders" to prevent the disease being brought in by passengers on planes and liners.

**Sunday 14**    "**Five Confirmed Smallpox Cases in Bradford**". More than 20,000 people vaccinated. Another suspected case is a pathologist who had performed the post-mortem examination of a girl who had died of smallpox. The female prisoners and staff of Strangeways Prison Hospital, Manchester, were vaccinated as a member of staff had been present in court when the pathologist was giving evidence.

---

### HERE IN BRITAIN

**"Horror Way Code"**

A police chief produced his own Highway Code to bring home to children that death is lurking on the roads.

The book, based on the official Highway Code, is full of sketches meant to horrify.

The author, Chief Constable of Derbyshire wrote the Code because the county had a record number of 130 road deaths last year.

---

### AROUND THE WORLD

**"Peru- Avalanche Entombs Nine Villages"**

Hundreds of people were killed and many more missing.

One of the best rescue dogs in the world was called in from Amsterdam to help the mercy work. He is Roy Roland, a four-year old Alsatian who is expert at finding and rescuing people trapped in snow, ruined buildings and rubble. He saved eight people from collapsed houses in a Belgian village last February.

# GERMANS PAY FOR TROOPS

The British Army of the Rhine was formed in August 1945 to defend and support the military government of the British zone of Allied-occupied Germany. As the potential threat of Soviet invasion across the North German Plain into West Germany increased, BAOR became more responsible for the defence of West Germany than its occupation.

The end of the Cold War resulted in BAOR being reduced in size, and in 1994 it became the 25,000 strong British Forces Germany (BFG). Following the 2010 Strategic Defence and Security Review, the permanent deployment of British Army units in Germany began to be phased out, with the last military base handed back to the German Bundeswehr in February 2020.

On Wednesday January 10th, Prime Minister Mr Macmillan flew home with a promise from West German Chancellor, Dr Adenauer, to help with the cost of maintaining British troops in Germany. One form of assistance will be the stepping up of German arms purchases from Britain considerably.

The West German Chancellor and the Premier also agreed in the talks that a committee of junior ministers from both countries should enquire into other ways of helping Britain to ease this drain on foreign currency reserves. Britain's Rhine army costs £70 million a year. It is believed that Mr Macmillan asked the Germans to provide more than £50 million this year. No figures were given in the communiqué issued after the tour which were described as full of understanding and real cordiality. However a Bonn government spokesman said there was agreement, by and large, on upper and lower limits.

The committee - brought into being largely on Mr Macmillan's initiative – will draw up a plan to pump desperately needed West German Marks into the British Treasury and will meet first in Bonn later this month. Measures may include more training facilities for German troops in Britain, a German contribution to British arms development and a German takeover of the Rhine Army's civilian wage bill.

# JANUARY 15TH - 21ST 1962

## IN THE NEWS

**Monday 15** — "**Civil Servants Go Slow**" Pressure for more action. By the end of this week, unions representing more than 380,000 of the 650,000 non-industrial civil servants will have members working to rule. Post office workers, Civil Service Clerical workers and Post Office Engineers will ban overtime and in their quest for improved pay and conditions.

**Tuesday 16** — "**Smallpox Under Control. Mass Vaccination Unnecessary**" announces the Ministry of Health. Emergency mass vaccination was not needed as the measures already put in place kept the outbreak contained.

**Wednesday 17** — "**RSPCA in New Storm Over Fox Hunting**". Results of a ballot showed that members of the RSPCA were overwhelmingly opposed to fox hunting. The RSPCA had warned members to ignore the ballot carried out by their rival, 'The League Against Cruel Sports', as whilst it opposed all forms of hunting for sport, they felt the alternative methods of control of foxes involved more suffering.

**Thursday 18** — "**Bishops Say Stop Hanging**". Bishops urged that the death penalty should be abolished, or at least, suspended for five years. They called for non capital punishment instead.

**Friday 19** — "**Lord Snowdon to be the Artistic Director**" to the Sunday Times. Mr Tony Armstrong Jones's decision to take a paid job has been widely attacked by the media.

**Saturday 20** — "**Russia Leaves Berlin to Wither on the Vine**". There will be no separate peace treaty between Russia and East Germany this year even as Soviet tanks left the divided city.

**Sunday 21** — "**Communist Jet Crashes Near Italian Missile Base**". Rolls of film taken from a plane are being closely guarded as they are believed to reveal why an airman from Communist Bulgaria crashed his Russian built MiG plane near a Western Alliance airbase in Italy.

## HERE IN BRITAIN

### "I Won't Be Lady Nina"
### Says The Junk Dealer's Daughter.

After a six-week romance, Nina Hobbs broke off her engagement to a peer's nephew because, "He didn't pay me enough attention, he was much more interested in model aeroplanes." Chain smoking in a room behind her father's shop, she said, "The wedding is off for good. Even when I was in the room with him, he didn't seem to notice!

One of the things we argued about was children, he wanted them, but I knew they would ruin my figure. Heavens, he even expected me to cook for him! I'm not that sort of girl!"

## AROUND THE WORLD

### "Cape Canaveral : It Is Space Week "

Marine Colonel John Glenn will climb into a phone booth sized Space ship ... and attempt to orbit the Earth three times.

American scientists need information from Glenn's flight to help design their Gemini two-man Space ship. America is prepared to spend £50 million building a fleet of Geminis to enable men to stay in orbit for a week or more.

The first Gemini flight is planned for late 1963 and is closely tied up with the Apollo project, designed to take three men to the Moon for one orbit before returning to Earth.

# ROYAL HUSBAND GETS A JOB

What a fuss about Tony Armstrong Jones, the husband of Princess Margaret, taking a paid job as Artistic Director at the Sunday Times which is owned by Mr Roy Thomson, a Canadian millionaire.

The foremost critic is The Observer, edited by the Hon. David Aster who moans that Mr Jones is a "major financial asset" to Mr Thomson. So why did he not offer the job himself?

Another testy critic is Lord Beaverbrook, also a Canadian millionaire who owns the Sunday Express and Evening Standard, who regards it all as a "gimmick". The editor of the Times, self-appointed keeper of the Royal Conscience, does not approve either.

The Daily Mirror, however, is in full support and says the criticism is sour and stuffy nonsense. "Mr Jones has found work where his talents as a photographer will find an outlet and says,

*"This young man will now be more usefully employed*
*than in walking the regulation number of paces behind his sister-in-law and his wife!"*

If the fact that he has taken a paid job on a newspaper means a break with royal traditions, then so much the better. Some royal traditions need breaking. Who can seriously argue in the year 1962, when Queen Victoria has been dead for 61 years, that it is somehow offensive for the husband of a royal princess to work for a wage? The Mirror hopes he will not be put off by the clamour and that he will stick to his job, which he will do very well."

# JANUARY 22ND - 28TH 1962

## IN THE NEWS

**Monday 22**  "**Red Pilot Quizzed**". The young Bulgarian pilot who crashed in Italy is in hospital. Some reports say he brought the MiG plane down on purpose, but the Bulgarians deny this saying his fuel supply ran out and he landed in the nearest safe spot. They are demanding that the pilot be repatriated.

**Tuesday 23**  "**Marples Blocks Rail Wage Talks.**" Ernest Marples The Minister for Transport stepped right over the head of Dr. Beeching the £24,000 a year boss of British Railways, and said the present pay claims by the Unions MUST go to arbitration.

**Wednesday 24**  "**Charles is Going to Dad's Old School.**"  Prince Charles is going to Gordonstoun on the shores of the Moray Firth in Scotland, and it's going to be tough. Among the 380 boys are the sons of peers and dockers, rich men and fishermen.

**Thursday 25**  "**Ordeal with a Killer on the A6.**" Sitting in a wheelchair at the A6 murder enquiry, Valerie Storie told of a night of terror with a killer gunman. She said there was no doubt, James Hanratty "was the man who had shot Mike Gregsten and me."

**Friday 26**  "**Hero with a Swagger Stick.**" A British Major faced a Congo mob of several hundred mutinous troops in Katanga where nineteen European priests had been massacred. He brought off the daring rescue of the only survivor – with a punch on the nose.

**Saturday 27**  "**Up She Goes, Destination the Moon.**" American scientists successfully launched the third of their Ranger ships on a voyage to the moon. Alas, soon after take-off, they calculated that it would miss by 20,000-30,000 miles.

**Sunday 28**  "**The Perverse Princess and Tony.**" Returning to London, Princess Margaret and her husband were under fire for having left their two-month-old son at home with his nanny, as they flew off for a holiday in the Caribbean sunshine.

## HERE IN BRITAIN
### "A Kiss Ends Murder Bid Case".

In Bedford, Giovanni Verola was cleared of trying to murder his "Hysterically jealous wife" with enough poison to kill seventy-five people.

His wife and mother of their six-month-old baby – with another one of the way – said, as they kissed and made up, "I will try not to be jealous anymore."

Verola had put so much mercuric chloride in a saucepan of milk for his wife, that it had made a hole in the pan, but he said he had "only wanted to frighten her!"

## AROUND THE WORLD
### Trotsky Widow Dies In Exile

Leon Trotsky's wife Natalie died this week in Paris. She was at her revolutionary husband's side during the Russian Revolution and witnessed the power battle between him and Stalin after Lenin died.

She and her husband tried to escape the assassins travelling from Turkey to France to Norway to Mexico until Trotsky, founder of the Red Army, was assassinated in Mexico 21 years ago on Stalin's orders. Even after his death, his widow had to be heavily guarded as she knew too many of Soviet dictator's secrets.

# COLD SHOWERS FOR CHARLES

Prince Charles, the Prince of Wales, is to go to Gordonstoun school where his father, the Duke of Edinburgh, went before him. Along with sons of the wealthy, the school has workers' sons who are scholarship boys who get financial help from shipping companies and local authorities. Like them, Charles will be put through the toughest training course of any school in the world.

Whatever the weather, the 13 year-old Prince will get up at 7am and take a cold shower, then go for a run, wearing the school uniform of shorts and open necked shirts, in the 300 acre estate which is set among the coastal plane of Morayshire.

Before breakfast he will do his household chores including cleaning out drains, sweeping his dormitory and cutting wood. His studies will include sailing, climbing rocks and mountains and back breaking organized expeditions. The emphasis will be on making a 'man of him' rather than an academic.

The principle which Gordonstoun emphasises is trust, "Under its influence boys cease to be mere objects of education and learn to make demands upon themselves. A sense of rivalry has to be encouraged and a boy must be led to discover something in which he can excel."

Gordonstoun was founded in 1935 by Dr. Kurt Hahn who was a leading sponsor of the Outward Bound Sea School at Aberdovey.

# JAN 29TH - FEB 4TH 1962

## IN THE NEWS

**Monday 29** "**All This and Monday Too!**" Buses will run normally. Underground trains will be heavily cut or OFF altogether. This is the prospect facing Londoners and others in the South as they set off for work today – transport's Black Monday.

**Tuesday 30** "**London Traffic Choked to a Standstill.**" Rush hour commuters switched to cars because of the tube and train strikes. Massive traffic jams caused chaos as thousands of motorists tried to struggle out of the City. Work to rule delays on the rails are to continue.

**Wednesday 31** "**Beat Jams, Work at Home.**" Scotland Yard traffic chief put forward a "startling plan" to beat the road chaos facing London again if there is a second tube strike. He urged firms to let a quarter of their staff work at home.

**Thurs 1ˢᵗ Feb** "**Out Again Next Monday.**" Unofficial leaders of the London Underground workers last night voted in favour of repeating the one-day shut down. Bus drivers may be asked to stage a 'sympathy stoppage' – which they did *not* do last Monday.

**Friday 2** "**Tory MPs Hit at Macmillan.**" The Prime Minister was criticised by his back bench MPs last night for his failure to "Tell the People" the reasons for the 'Pay Pause' and had therefore failed to get the Nation's support for the Government's economic measures.

**Saturday 3** "**Booing Students Jeer at Prime Minister.**" A crowd of booing undergraduates and Campaign for Nuclear Disarmament supporters surrounded Mr. Macmillan at Oxford and barred his entrance to the Oxford Union debating hall for five minutes.

**Sunday 4** "**Wales Scotched.**" Scotland beat Wales at rugby yesterday 8-3 in a rip-roaring match, making it the Scots' first win at Cardiff Arms Park in thirty five years.

## HERE IN BRITAIN

**"The Queen Buys A King-Size Yacht."**
The Queen and the Duke of Edinburgh have bought Bloodhound, an ocean racing yawl. The 63ft long Bloodhound, one of the world's most famous yachts, is believed to have cost them about £10,000 and is to replace their 29ft long Dragon class yacht Bluebottle, which was a wedding present from the Island Sailing Club at Cowes, Isle of Wight.

When not required by the Royal Family, Bloodhound will be on loan to yachting clubs for cruises, regattas and "some ocean racing."

## AROUND THE WORLD

**"Automation As A Cause Of Unrest."**
A USA study of the effect of computers and automation has concluded that their widespread use may create vast unemployment and social unrest, which could seriously weaken the foundations of a free society and lead to new Luddite wars.

Regarded as inevitable because of its economic advantages, cybernation will bring widespread unemployment especially among untrained adolescents resulting in a surfeit of leisure and rise of delinquency.

# END OF WORLD HELD UP

The outlook for India where millions of Hindus were expecting the end of the world to start yesterday was rather brighter this morning.

Astrologers had predicted a weekend of disasters beginning when the moon entered the Zodiac sign of Capricorn at noon [British time] yesterday.

Holy men throughout the country led mass prayer-meetings at the approach of the dreaded conjunction of Sun, Moon, Earth and the planets Mercury, Venus, Mars, Jupiter and Saturn.

In New Delhi, men, women and children gathered in temples and on the banks of the river to ask the Goddess of Destruction to take pity on mankind.

Then came a last-minute note of optimism from one of the country's best-known astrologers. He said the Moon had suddenly begun a "drift" from Capricorn – which boded well for India and Asia. Western countries were though, he added ominously, still in danger when there is a total eclipse of the Sun in the Pacific area tomorrow.

Despite scientific assurances that nothing would happen, hundreds of New Delhi office workers asked for time off, but throughout the period of supplication to the gods, Prime Minister Nehru has ridiculed the prophets of doom and gone on steadfastly with his election campaign tour.

## IN THE NEWS

**Monday 5**    **"Underground Trains to Run."** Today's London underground strike will not take place as the drivers who had been working to rule will end their campaign at midnight.

**Tuesday 6**    **"Dr Beeching Offers Railwaymen 3%."** The Chairman of British Railways defied the Government's request for arbitration and offered more than their pay cap of 2.5%, but still it gained an unfavourable response from Union leaders.

**Wednesday 7**    **"Owners Resist 500 Power Pylons."** Over 70 landowners are objecting to 78 miles of pylons to take nuclear power from Sizewell in Suffolk to Luton, Bedfordshire.

**Thursday 8**    **"Hanratty Tells Jury he Made a Terrible Mistake"** by lying to the detective as to his whereabouts on the night of the A6 Murder. His counsel asks, "Is He the Monster?"

**Friday 9**    **"Indictable Offences in London Up by 12,000."** With robberies in London up by a quarter last year, a new and urgent appeal to the public to help halt the serious rise in crime was issued yesterday by the Police Commissioner.

**Saturday 10**    **"Prime Minister Harold Macmillan celebrates 68th birthday"** with his wife, Lady Dorothy Macmillan, at his home, Birch Grove in Sussex.

**Sunday 11**    **"Bardot is Terror Target."** In response to a letter from the OAS Terrorist Group demanding 50,000 francs, she stood In front of her film crew in Britain, Brigitte Bardot raised her right arm and publicly repeated, "I swear that I shall fight to the death against Fascism."

### HERE IN BRITAIN

**"It's Third Time Lucky for Dora."**

Dora Bryan proudly presented her newest co-star, William John, to the press at a Hove, Sussex, nursing home.

Dora, 38, lost her first two babies. She and husband Bill Lawton, the Lancashire League cricketer, have two adopted children, Daniel, aged 3, and 17 month old Georgina. They live in Brighton.

Dora, instantly recognisable from her voice, which has become a trademark of her performances, has starred in many theatrical productions and her films include *"The Cockleshell Heroes"*, *"Carry on Sergeant"* and *"A Taste of Honey"*.

### AROUND THE WORLD

**"Angry Cuban Reply to USA Trade Embargo."**

The Cuban Government has reacted swiftly and angrily to President Kennedy's ban on United States trade with Cuba and thousands of Cubans have gathered from all parts of the island into Havana for a protest rally.

President Kennedy's proclamation issued this week forbids all trade with Cuba (including the import of all goods emanating from Cuba) no matter how they might be sent toward the US, except that on humanitarian grounds some food and medicine will continue to be sent to the island.

# BARDOT FIGHTS FASCISM

*A 1962 march against the OAS with Brigitte Bardot (in the inset photo)*

Brigitte Bardot, France's No 1 'sex kitten' star, this week publicly defied the murderous, French, Right Wing Secret Army [OAS]. Standing among film technicians at the Billancourt Studios in Paris, she raised her right arm and solemnly repeated the oath: "I swear that I will fight to the death against Fascism." The Secret Army who are fanatically opposed to President de Gaulle's policy of independence for Algeria, are terrorising Paris with bomb blasts and Brigitte will undoubtedly become a prime target for them.

Brigitte recently refused to knuckle down to the Secret Army when they demanded £3,600 from her last month – and infuriated them by having their letter published in a left-wing political magazine. Since then, her home has been under constant police guard to prevent any attempt to blow it up.

One of her friends said tonight, "We are worried that she is openly not only defying the terrorists but trying to encourage others to do so. She is already a marked woman and after today she will surely be in even greater danger."

On Saturday 10 February, all over Paris, work came to a halt for an hour as thousands of workers joined a protest strike against the OAS and for freedom for Algeria.

# FEBRUARY 12TH - 18TH 1962

## IN THE NEWS

**Monday 12**   "**Operation on the Prince of Wales.**" Thirteen-year-old Prince Charles was taken to Great Ormond Street Hospital early this morning and operated on for appendicitis. His condition is now satisfactory.

**Tuesday 13**   "**Call for End to Arms Race.**" A letter from Mr. Macmillan and President Kennedy, sent to the Soviet leader Mr. Khrushchev, emphasized the need for a supreme effort at the forthcoming disarmament negotiations.

**Wednesday 14**   "**Mr. Khrushchev Steps up Pressure.**" His plans to turn the Geneva conference into an 18 Nation Summit received a cool reception but he plans to go ahead anyway, even if Macmillan and US President Kennedy stay away.

**Thursday 15**   "**Trend Against the Death Penalty.**" But there will be no bid yet to alter the law as the Government is "not radical enough" to amend the Homicide Act 1957 which allows for death by hanging for the murder of police and prison officers, for causing

**Friday 16**   "**Peace as Railmen take 7d.**" The Unions agreed to Dr Beeching's final pay rise offer of 3% which equals 7d (2.5p) in the £. This will take effect when the Government's pay pause ends in April.

**Saturday 17**   "**The Shattered City.**" Gales reaching 177mph ripped across Britain yesterday killing eleven people and shattering Sheffield, Britain's steel capital.

**Sunday 18**   "**Prime Minister to Discuss Sheffield Storm Aid.**" Following a 30 mile tour of stricken areas, Dr Hill the Minister for Housing and Local Government, is to discuss the amount of Government aid available for the City's storm damaged property.

## HERE IN BRITAIN

### "The Dog Who Must Not Smoke."

Butch, a dog with a craving for cigarettes, has been put under a no-smoking ban at two pubs in Doncaster.

His owner, a local timber merchant, said yesterday, "I've been expecting this. The other customers in the pubs give him cigarettes because they like to see him smoke, but when he comes to the end of a cigarette, he just spits it out – and lighted dog ends can be dangerous!"

## AROUND THE WORLD

### "Corned Beef KO's Liz Taylor."

Film star Elizabeth Taylor was recovering from food poisoning in a Rome clinic last night. The cause of the trouble: a tin of corned beef.

Liz, 29, who has the title role in the multi-million-dollar film *"Cleopatra"* ate the meat at lunch with her producer, who also had mild food poisoning, and was rushed to the clinic after fainting at her villa. Liz's husband, American singer Eddie Fisher flew back from Portugal where he was working, to visit her in the clinic. Her illness will not delay shooting on the film set.

# RECORD GALES BLAST BRITAIN

After a swathe of destructive gales swept the country early in the week, the terror of a typhoon hit Britain on Friday, killing eleven people, wrecking homes, schools and factories and leaving a trail of misery, orphans and heartbreak in its wake.

One gust on the Isle of Unst in the North Shetlands reached 177mph – the highest ever recorded in Britain.

In Sheffield 200 people were injured and 500 made homeless when, of 163,000 houses in the city, 70,000 were damaged and 98 demolished. One eye witness recalled, "Power lines were flashing and it was so noisy that all the family got up and sat drinking tea. I remember mum saying it was just like the Blitz. As daylight came, you could see all the devastation. Chimney stacks were down and bits of roof were missing."

The youngest fatality was 17-year-old John William Johnson who died in his bed. Rescuers could not get to him because part of the upstairs floor had collapsed. Vicar's wife Shirley Hill, aged 30, died after being trapped in her Brightside home by a falling chimney and Ida Stabbs, aged 57, was killed in bed in Crookes. A fourth person, Edward Wadsworth, of Shafton, Barnsley, who was hit by falling masonry, died.

All over the north, roads were blocked by fallen trees and hundreds of telephone lines were down. Lorries and vans were blown off the road and at sea, ships raced for shelter. At Huddersfield's home football ground, two 144ft floodlight towers crashed down and two were left tottering.

# FEBRUARY 19TH - 25TH 1962

## IN THE NEWS

**Monday 19**
"**Hanratty Found Guilty.**" James Hanratty was convicted on Saturday of the A6 murder and announced last night he will appeal. With pressure to abolish the death penalty, if the appeal is dismissed, will he hang?

**Tuesday 20**
"**Soviet insists on Berlin Air Rights.**" Mr. Khrushchev says the allies do NOT have unrestricted access to the air corridors between Berlin and the West. Britain, America and France have complained of Soviet MiGs harassing allied flights.

**Wednesday 21**
"**Glenn the Space Hero.**" John Glenn has orbited the Earth three times. From launching to splash down in the Caribbean, he had been 4 hours 56 minutes in the air.

**Thursday 22**
"**Let's GO Together.**" Mr. Khrushchev's suggestion that America and Russia should pool their efforts to explore outer space got a swift answer. President Kennedy said "Yes".

**Friday 23**
"**Secret 'Peace' Talks for ITV.**" Two small teams from Equity and 13 independent television companies are talking in a bid to end the actors' 16 week pay strike.

**Saturday 24**
"**Well Done John.**" Space conqueror John Glenn received a roaring welcome from a crowd of 100,000 when he was decorated by President Kennedy for his bravery and skill.

**Sunday 25**
"**No, No, Says Kennedy.**" Mr. Macmillan urged the President to be "more flexible" as Mr. Khrushchev's *second* call for Summit level talks on disarmament were rejected in America.

## HERE IN BRITAIN

**"Acquitted – Because He Smoked Too Much".**
A motorist claimed that his smoker's cough was responsible for the 'trail of havoc' he caused– *and he won his case.*

A specialist defending the 50-a-day-man said, "It is well known that coughing due to smoking can cause a temporary black-out."

The magistrates accepted that this was the reason why the man's car had mounted the footpath on the wrong side of the road, injured a pedestrian, bent a no-waiting sign and wrecked a shop window before embedding itself in the walls of a public house so hard that it dislodged a fireplace.

The driver was not injured!

## AROUND THE WORLD

**"The Dancing Major Dies At 43"**
In Cairo, Major Saleh Salem, the "voice of Egypt" under Nasser until 1955 and the so called "dancing major", has died.

Dapper but turbulent, he came to power in 1952 when King Farouk was overthrown and earned his nickname when he joined Sudanese tribesmen in a ceremonial dance in his underpants. He called himself Britain's Public Enemy No 1 during the Suez crisis saying his people would blow up the canal if Egypt were invaded.

Yet it was to British medical skill that he owed the last years of his life, his kidney disease was treated in the London Clinic by the Queen's Physician, and by transfusions of English blood!

# EUROPE REJECTS BRITAIN

*The EU has two headquarters, one in Brussels and the other in Strasbourg. Members of the Commission travel between the two sites on a regular basis. There are sub offices in Spain, Germany and Italy.*

Since Britain applied last year to join the European Economic Community – the regional organization to bring about economic integration among its member states - she has been given a first taste of the tough treatment to expect in the food and agriculture section of the Common Market negotiations.

The six original members (Belgium, France, Germany, Italy, Luxembourg and the Netherlands) of the Market say that Britain cannot be given longer than seven and a half years to adjust herself to the Market's farm policy.

This was in response to a speech by Mr Christopher Soames, Minister of Agriculture, in which he told the Six that Britain accepted the general principles and framework of the policy but because this would force us to make a lot of modifications to our present food policy, he asked that Britain should be given twelve years to adjust the nation to the new conditions.

He said that Britain's transition to the Common Market farm system must be very gradual in order to safeguard our farmers. British housewives must have time to get used to higher food prices and Commonwealth food producers should be given guaranteed markets for their produce in Europe and the chance to find new ones elsewhere.

Mr Soames said the British system of having an annual review of farm prices and policy could, and should, be grafted on the Common Market system.

# FEB 26TH - MARCH 4TH 1962

## IN THE NEWS

**Monday 26** "**US to Continue Berlin Flights – Whatever Happens.**" Following the Soviet interventions, US flights to Berlin through the air corridors will continue even if it means substituting commercial with military aircraft.

**Tuesday 27** "**Snow and Frost Tighten Grip. Cold Weather to Continue.**" Snow fell nearly everywhere in England, Scotland and Wales and temperatures remain below freezing.

**Wednesday 28** "**Last Hope Flight**." Sir Roy Welensky, Premier of the Federation of Rhodesia & Nyasaland, flew to London for a last hope battle with the Government to keep white supremacy in the Federation.

**Thurs 1st March** "**Use of Force.**" Sir Roy Welensky threatened force in response to the proposed changes to the Rhodesian constitution put forward by Mr Maudling the Colonial Secretary.

**Friday 2** "**30-Second Jet Disaster – 95 Killed.**" A Boeing 707 nose-dived into a swamp thirty seconds after taking off from New York's Idlewild Airport.

**Saturday3** "**£70 Return Fares to Cross Atlantic.**" A plan to revive falling sea traffic across the Atlantic is to increase inclusive tours and reduce the current package fares by half.

**Sunday 4** "**Blizzard Air Crash.**" A pilot father and his two children, on a 'Sunday Flip', were killed yesterday when his light aircraft flew into a blizzard and crashed in Yorkshire.

## HERE IN BRITAIN

**"Walkers Must Obey The Lights."**

It was announced in the Commons by Transport Minister, Ernest Marples, that pedestrians, like motorists, will be prosecuted if they "cross on the red" during a new push-button traffic-light experiment in London area.

Pedestrians will be able to use the push-button system to stop traffic in all directions whilst they cross, but when the lights are against them, they must wait – even if nothing is coming.

They will be liable to prosecution if they disobey, and it will also be an offence to cross these roads at any point other than the lights.

## AROUND THE WORLD

**"Troops Fire in 2 Hours Of Casbah Terror."**

A fierce battle between French troops and rooftop snipers took place in the Casbah, the old Muslim quarter of Algiers.

The vast honeycomb of shanties, in which 80,000 Muslims live crowded together, was surrounded by hundreds of troops after a French private had been stabbed to death.

More than 50 people died at the end of one of the bloodiest weeks of terrorism of the war and one which has made grim mockery of the laborious approach to a cease-fire.

Peace is still no closer despite attempts to organise final Franco-Algerian peace talks.

# SIR ROY JETS TO LONDON

*A BOAC Comet With Sir Roy Welensky (Inset)*

Sir Roy, the ex-boxer Premier of the Federation of Rhodesia and Nyasaland set off suddenly from Salisbury, Southern Rhodesia after reading the formal text of Britain's new proposals for Northern Rhodesia's political future.

There was no scheduled flight to London, but a British Overseas Airways Corporation Comet was about to fly across Southern Rhodesia on its way to London from Johannesburg. Comets do not normally stop at Salisbury, but Sir Roy asked that this one "pick him up"! It was agreed by BOAC headquarters in London and the pilot was told by radio to land at Salisbury. Sir Roy was driven at top speed to the airport and right onto the tarmac where he boarded the plane.

In the meantime, Prime Minister Mr Macmillan was stating that he would not be proposing that Sir Roy visited London at the present time!

Sir Roy will be in London to hear the Colonial Secretary, Mr Maudling, tell the Commons about the Government's revised proposals for a new Northern Rhodesian Constitution. It is understood that the proposals make reasonably certain the election of an African Nationalist, 'anti-Welensky', majority to the local Parliament. Their aim being to take Northern Rhodesia out of the Federation.

# MARCH 5TH - 11TH 1962

## IN THE NEWS

**Monday 5**  "**Factory Gates Close for One-Day Strike.**" Nearly 3 Million engineering and shipyard workers stage a 24 hour strike in protest at the rejection of a pay & hours demand.

**Tuesday 6**  "**Forces Pay Shock.**" Forces pay is to go up next month but the Government has broken its promise to keep it in line with "Civvy Street" pay.

**Wednesday 7**  "**Primate to Russia**." The Archbishop of Canterbury, Dr Michael Ramsey, is to go to Moscow. It will be the first visit by an Archbishop.

**Thursday 8**  "**The Crash of U2.**" Gary Powers, the US pilot, tells for the first time the story of his struggle to exit the Spy plane when it was disabled over Soviet airspace in 1960.

**Friday 9**  "**Prime Minister's EEC Denial.**" Mr Macmillan firmly denied that the Government had given any impression that they were "going to get into the Common Market at any price."

**Saturday 10**  "**Little Men Beat the ICI Giant.**" Britain's biggest takeover battle fizzled out when Imperial Chemical Industries gained control of only one third of the shares of Courtaulds, the textiles manufacturer.

**Sunday 11**  "**Man Dies, Scores Hurt in Soccer Drama**" when railings collapsed during yesterday's Sheffield Utd. v Burnley FA Cup Quarter Final match at Sheffield.

## HERE IN BRITAIN

### "It May Fetch A Million"

One of the world's most valuable pictures is to be sold to provide an endowment fund to help pay the cost of training Britain's young artists. The picture is a drawing of the Virgin and Child by Leonardo Da Vinci and is owned by the Royal Academy of Art.

The Academy's president commented, "The decision to part with the drawing was not an easy one, it is a world-famous masterpiece entirely by the hand of Leonardo himself and has been preserved in good condition by the Academy for at least 183 years. But we need the money and are hoping someone may bid up to £1million, the highest sum ever paid for a work of art."

## AROUND THE WORLD

### "Paris Terror Blast."

On Friday, Paris was stunned by the city's latest and biggest terrorist bomb outrage. A car bomb standing outside a meeting hall exploded. Two policemen and a caretaker were killed instantly.

Fifty other people, some of who were delegates to a 'peace conference' and some passengers in a bus that was battered by flying debris, were wounded.

The bomb is assumed to have been planted by the Right-Wing Secret Army the OAS which is fanatically opposed to Independence for Algeria. "The struggle against the OAS was one of the subjects on the agenda at the peace conference.

# US SPY PLANE SHOT DOWN

Gary Powers is an American pilot whose Central Intelligence Agency [CIA] Lockheed U2 plane was shot down while he was flying a reconnaissance mission in Soviet Union airspace on May 1st, 1960. The U2 was equipped with a state-of-the-art camera designed to take high-resolution photos of military installations and other important sites in hostile countries including the Soviet Union. This week he gave his own dramatic account of the mission that made him Russia's prisoner for two years.

Speaking calmly, in a matter-of-fact manner, he said that while he was flying from his base in Turkey across Russia, he spotted vapour trails of aircraft well below him. As he wheeled at heights of 68,000 feet, he suddenly saw a bright orange light all around him and the aircraft's controls went 'limp' meaning he could not manoeuvre it properly.

He said he heard what he thought was an explosion in the rear of the plane and thought the tail had come off and then thought the wings had come off too. He was trapped inside the cockpit, plunging towards the earth and tried to fire the mechanism that would destroy the plane.

The blast that wrecked the plane is believed to have been caused by a Soviet missile which blew up without scoring a direct hit. Holding a model of the U2, Mr Powers said that if he had fired the ejection seat to clear himself, he would have cut off both his legs below the knee where they had become wedged under the instrument panel.

Half in and half out of the plane, he tried desperately to destroy the cameras but could not reach the button. He eventually managed to jerk himself free and almost immediately his parachute opened and he floated to the ground where he was captured.

# MARCH 12TH - 18TH 1962

## IN THE NEWS

**Monday 12**    "**Baby is Smallpox Victim.**" The toll in the Rhondda Valley smallpox epidemic rose to four last night with the death of a baby girl. The number of people in isolation hospitals rose to twenty-three.

**Tuesday 13**    "**Cambridge Students in Marijuana Probe.**" Six people, believed to have organized a "reefer" ring amongst the students, are being hunted by detectives. Police are concerned by the rise in illegal drug taking by students

**Wednesday 14**    "**ITV Peace Hopes Rise.**" Equity, the actors' union will meet the ITV companies tomorrow in a new attempt to end the actor's pay strike, now in its fifth month.

**Thursday 15**    "**Tony Wants Car Hotted Up.**" Tony Armstrong Jones arranged with Alec Issigonis the chief designer of his Mini-Cooper, to have it modified to reach a speed of 95mph.

**Friday 16**    "**Hanratty Execution Date.**" The execution of James Hanratty the A6 killer has been fixed for April 4th at Bedford Prison. His appeal against conviction has been dismissed.

**Saturday 17**    "**Global Rocket Claim by Mr Khrushchev.**" Russia has developed a new "global rocket" which it claims is "invulnerable to anti-rocket weapons".

**Sunday 18**    "**Germans to Pay £108 million.**" The West German Government has made an offer of £54m over the next two years towards the upkeep of British Army of the Rhine.

## HERE IN BRITAIN
### "Petrol Down Soon"

The big oil companies are planning to cut the price of petrol. This is expected to be the first of two or three petrol price cuts similar to those made in 1960.

Then the companies made two reductions of 1/2d a gallon and one of 1d a gallon. But last year the Government more than cancelled this out by putting on an extra 3d a gallon in tax.

There are two main reasons behind the cuts now being planned:
1. A surplus of crude oil has led to a fall in crude oil prices and
2. A surplus of oil tankers which means they can be chartered by oil companies at lower rates.

## AROUND THE WORLD
### "Device to Calm Seas By 'Wave Traps'"

A 'wave trap' invention has been made public by the United States Rubber Company.

The wave traps consist of vertical panels of rubber-coated fabric hanging from plastic foam-rubber floats which ride on the water.

Scientists believe large versions could quell waves of 10ft. or higher. Potential uses include protecting ocean shores from erosion by wave action; creating calm seas for diving, rescue and refuelling operations and protecting off-shore oil rigs.

The lab based invention now needs to be tested in the sea.

# DOPING SCARE AT RACES

A guard to stop "nobblers" will travel with 'Another Flash', odds on favourite for the £5,000 plus Champion Hurdle at Cheltenham races, as the horse is driven thirty miles to the course.

The trainer ordered the special watch on the horse after three men picked a lock and broke into his stables at lonely Guys Cliffe, near Warwick, early yesterday. The men were foiled by two stable lads who chased them off. The lads were keeping an eve-of-the-race watch on 'Scottish Memories' the 2-1 favourite beaten at that day's National Hunt Championship Chase and 'Another Flash' was in the box next door. A passage with an outside door leads to the boxes. The men picked the lock of this door, but the Lads heard them and rushed out. The intruders ran 'like scalded cats' and escaped by car.

Within minutes the police arrived in squad cars from Warwick, two miles away, and searched the seventy-acre training establishment where thirty valuable horses are trained, but it was too late.

'Another Flash', who was declared none the worse for the incident, has won all his five races this season and he will be ridden in the Champion Hurdle by Bobby Beasley, the winner of last year's Grand National.

In a previous doping scare, detectives were given a description of a mystery woman, dressed in black and speaking with a foreign accent, who called at Guys Cliffe inquiring about placing a horse for training. Other trainers later reported visits from a similar woman before attempts were made to "get at" horses.

# MARCH 19TH - 25TH 1962

## IN THE NEWS

**Monday 19**    "**Cease Fire in Algeria.**" The bloody seven-year war officially ends today. But the outlawed Secret Army say, "We will fight on."

**Tuesday 20**    "**Train Crash Atom Alert.**" A box of radio-active material from Harwell Atomic Research Station was broken in a rail crash near Newcastle.

**Wednesday 21**    "**Ban the Smokers Bid in London, Bristol and Manchester.**" Councils move to ban smoking in cinemas, theatres, dance halls and on public transport.

**Thursday 22**    "**French Fire on the French.**" In Algeria, French security forces clashed with the Secret Army [OAS] for the first time in a pitched battle.

**Friday 23**    "**Explosion at Hapton Valley Colliery, Burnley.**" 16 Miners were killed and a further 21 injured in an explosion deep underground. "There was a terrible blast and we were all blown 10 or 15 yards along the face", said Mr. Jack Murray, aged 36, senior man of the 90 fillers who were shovelling coal on their hands and knees.

**Saturday 24**    "**H-Jet Crash Kills Four.**" The bomber plunged into a Lincolnshire farmhouse kitchen killing the farmer's wife and housekeeper and two members of the crew.

**Sunday 25**    "**De Gaulle Declares War on Secret Army.**" In Algeria, his troops surrounded the OAS stronghold of Bab-el-Oued with the aim to "starve them out."

## HERE IN BRITAIN

### "Ice 'Ghosts' Make A Cool £3,000"

To people with a taste for crime, the idea of 'ghost' workers at an ice-cream factory was the flavour of the month. Eight new workers were brought in by staff conspirators for the "high season" and each received £10 but not one of them turned up to work. On record they were the best workers any firm could have!

They were never late ... someone always clocked in for them. They were never sick ... they could not go on sick pay. They never caused any industrial disputes ... they would have been involved in any following inquiries.

The conspiracy was found out after six months but in that time the 'ghosts' had earned £3,000 which went into the eight conspirators' own pockets.

## AROUND THE WORLD

### "German Call To Make Duelling Illegal"

German university professors have written to the Bundestag asking members to make duelling, including its more inoffensive traditional student variety, the *Mensur,* a punishable offence.

Until about 1933 duelling in Germany was not regarded as an ordinary criminal offence but a question of honour and was punishable by 'honourable' imprisonment in a fortress. Since then it has been made punishable with ordinary imprisonment up to a maximum of five years if there is deliberate intent to kill.

The Federal High Court has ruled on several occasions that it is not contrary to morals and therefore not punishable under the German code.

# ROYALTY HITS OUT

*Prince Philip In Brazil 1962*

Prince Phillip has dynamited the Royal Tradition sky high when he blew his top in Rio de Janeiro. He accused Lord Beaverbrook of publishing:

    1. A "bloody awful newspaper." 2. A newspaper "full of lies." 3. A newspaper "full of scandal." Furthermore, and for good measure in case anybody missed the point, he accused Lord Beaverbrook of publishing a "vicious newspaper." In each case, the Prince was referring to the Daily Express.

The Duke has used the word "bloody" before – and why not he was a sailor after all? But has Royalty the right to reply to criticisms published about Royalty for the public to read!
Prince Philip was, not to put too fine a point on it, expressing his anger at the attacks on himself in particular and on Royalty in general by Beaverbrook's minions, especially John Gordon the Editor in Chief of the Sunday Express.

The Daily Mirror said, *"Prince Philip is completely within his bloody rights and good luck to him!"*, The Mirror was saying, *"He has set a fine example, let us have some more outspoken replies from the Palace instead of the flabby 'officialese' which is usually issued. "*

If members of the Royal Family feel offended or hurt by newspaper criticism, why should they not reply? If reports are wrong, or if rumours are published as fact, it is only fair that Royalty should have the right to issue denials or disclaimers.

While Prince Philip goes so far as to express his views in quarterdeck language – perhaps the Queen herself, or even the Queen Mother, should denounce a lie as a "jolly bad show." Perhaps the Queen enjoyed a quiet chuckle when she read the oath delivered by her husband in Rio!

# IN THE NEWS

**Monday 26** — "**Snow**." Summer time started yesterday but in parts of northern Britain, cars and lorries were sliding on snow whilst the sun shone in the south.

**Tuesday 27** — "**Rail Fares to Rise**." Fares will go up by 2 shillings (10p) in the pound, just in time for the Whitsun family holidays!

**Wednesday 28** — "**TV Violence – Cabinet Calls for Inquiry**." Government probe triggered by the murder scene in "Oliver Twist" shown on BBC Children's TV.

**Thursday 29** — "**More Merseyside Dockers on Strike**." In the second week of a dispute over Unions, more than 10,000 men were out in Liverpool, Birkenhead and Garston.

**Friday 30** — "**Two Horses Die at Aintree**." In a day of "tumbles" on the day before the toughest steeplechase. The Grand National is run there tomorrow and there are fears that more horses will be injured or die as they tackle the massive fences.

**Saturday 31** — "**Prince Stays to Play Polo**." Prince Philip, touring South America, stayed on at a ranch near Buenos Aires whilst Argentina suffers in the grip of an Army revolt.

**Sun 1st April** — "**Stop Dumping Spare Milk**." Government urged to send surplus skimmed milk [left after butter making] to underfed people overseas rather than dumping it in disused coal pits.

## HERE IN BRITAIN

**"Plan For Submarine Cargoes Outlined."**

Plans for a nuclear-powered submarine cargo ship, designed to cross the Atlantic at high speed more than 250ft below the surface were outlined at the Royal Institution of Naval Architects in London.

The ship, which would have been the world's first big submarine cargo vessel was designed in 1958 to carry iron ore to Britain from northern Canada, travelling under ice for part of the voyage.

The project is not being proceeded with because "the economic advantages are, at the moment, debatable." But architects will continue to work in this field, "until, in due course, such a vessel becomes a successful reality."

## AROUND THE WORLD

**"Big Appetites Blamed For Food Shortages."**

"You see", the young and keen official from the agricultural section of an East German party office said, "there are still short-comings in our production of consumer goods. The farmers on the whole are making a lot of money but they cannot find much to spend it on except food.

People are eating too much in the German Democratic Republic. That is why there is not enough to go round. If there were more cars and refrigerators, they would spend their money on those."

He added, "Production has gone up very sharply but so has consumption and East Germany cannot afford to import food with the proceeds of her industrial production."

# Is TV Violence Too Much?

The Home Secretary will announce this week, an inquiry into television shows and violence on the screen. He has already had talks with the BBC and the Independent Television Authority, who are sharing the costs and the probe will be carried out by an independent panel.

Their brief will be to investigate not just the question of violence, but both the good and the bad effects of viewing in the home, learning how to make the best use of television for the benefit of viewers as a whole. However, they will be looking for any decline in moral standards it may have caused, taking into account the increase in juvenile crime. When published, the report will set out TVs benefits and disadvantages to serve as a blueprint for future programme development.

The storm in the Commons arose from questions about TV violence following the screening of a scene in BBC's "Oliver Twist" where Bill Sikes clubs his companion, Nancy, to death with a pistol. Even though a warning had been given in a trailer during the afternoon and at the start of the programme, the Postmaster-General who saw it for himself, still condemned it as brutal and inexcusable.

The producer of this version of Charles Dickens' book, said, "It is not a fairy tale. It is one of the most brutal and violent stories in English literature. Murder is real and horrible, and children have to learn the nasty facts of life."

In the final episode, Bill Sikes falls off a roof clinging to a rope – which tightens around his neck. This will be out of range of the TV cameras, but viewers will see the shadow of a body hanging from a rope.

# APRIL 2ND - 8TH 1962

## IN THE NEWS

**Monday 2** — **"ETU Sacks Communist Leaders."** Four former leaders of the Electrical Trades Union have been expelled by the anti-communist executive council for their part in last year's ballot rigging scandal.

**Tuesday 3** — **"ITV Strike Ends."** After 21 weeks, Equity members have gained huge increases in basic pay rates – and extra money when a show is "networked."

**Wednesday 4** — **"James Hanratty Hanged."** The 'A6 murderer', convicted of killing scientist Michael Gregsten, was hanged at 8am today at Bedford jail.

**Thursday 5** — **"Nurses March in Revolt."** More than 4,000 nurses marched through rain-swept London in protest against 'insulting' pay rise offer.

**Friday 6** — **"Tobacco Firms to Limit Advertising**." Six companies announced steps in an attempt to reduce the attraction of smoking to children.

**Saturday 7** — **"Duke of Edinburgh back from S. America."** After two months, eleven countries and 36,000 miles, Prince Philip arrived home and went straight to Windsor Castle to meet the Queen.

**Sunday 8** — **"More Smallpox Cases in Wales."** Eight women in a mental hospital in Bridgend, Glamorgan are suspected of having the disease.

## HERE IN BRITAIN

### "Fishing For Chips."

More than 700 fish and chip shops may soon say *"Frying tonight – but no chips."* Chip shop owners are facing a potato shortage which may last until next year's crops are available.

The crisis is particularly bad in South Wales where a spokesman for the National Federation of Fish Fryers said, "Can you imagine China without chop suey, Italy without spaghetti and Wales without chips?"

The Welsh eat 65% of the total potato tonnage in Britain and wholesale prices are higher because of the severe winter. Even schoolchildren are getting fewer spuds with their dinners because of the high prices!

## AROUND THE WORLD

### "Liz Taylor 'Says Marriage Is Over'"

Film star Elizabeth Taylor has said her three-year marriage to singer Eddie Fisher is "dead and gone," and has phoned her divorce lawyer to ask him to fly immediately to Rome where she is filming "Cleopatra."

Fisher, Liz's fourth husband said he had plans to leave New York for California "for quite some time."
Meanwhile in Rome, Liz went back on the "Cleopatra" set with her leading man, Welsh actor Richard Burton.

Her previous husbands were, in 1950 Conrad Hilton, heir to the hotel chain. 1952: actor Michael Wilding and 1957 film producer Mike Todd, who died in a plane crash a year later.

# TV STARS DOUBLE PAY

*The Tiller Girls At The London Palladium*

The five-month-old strike by Equity, the actors' union, against the Independent television companies, ended this week with a great stride forward for performers. The earnings of more than half the Equity members working in television would be trebled and of a fifth, doubled, costing the ITV companies about £2m a year. Actors have gained huge increases in basic pay rates – and extra money when a show is "networked" – used by more than one company.

Equity will now turn their attention to the BBC where another 5 shillings (25p) is expected to be added to the combined £4 television and radio licence if the BBC is to meet their demands, including the same terms for walk-ons and extras which ITV have agreed to.

The new agreement meets the demand that there should be a relationship between the fee paid and the area to which the performance is transmitted. There will be four such areas, London, the Midlands, the North, and the rest of the country – and a sum equal to the performance fee will be paid for each area to which the performance is transmitted.

Viewers can now look forward to seeing once more their favourite top shows: "Emergency Ward 10" and "Probation Officer" are likely to be the first to return within the month. The first big show to benefit by the settlement will be "Sunday Night at the London Palladium" which has kept running despite the strike, but it has had to do without Equity members.

Now comedian, Max Bygraves, who *is* a member, will be back to topping the Bill. The Tiller Girls dance troupe will be allowed to return as will Angela Bracewell, the hostess of the "Beat the Clock" game in the show. However, old films and other "standby shows" will have to go on for some weeks until programmes are reorganised.

# APRIL 9TH - 15TH 1962

## IN THE NEWS

**Monday 9**    "**Budget Day**." Mr Selwyn Lloyd slapped a new tax on sweets, soft drinks and ice-cream, but left the price of cigarettes untouched in spite of the accepted link between smoking and lung cancer.

**Tuesday 10**    "**Explosion in Gun Powder Factory.**" More than thirty men and women have died in the explosion which ripped apart the factory in south east France.

**Wednesday 11**    "**Margaret's Photo Sells Nappies.**" A photo Tony Armstrong Jones took of his wife Princess Margaret and their baby, has appeared on the cover of a French baby wear catalogue – proving a huge success.

**Thursday 12**    "**They All Want to be Croupiers.**" With the prospect of Britain's first legal casino [Betting & Gaming Act 1960] opening soon in Brighton, 1600 people have applied to work there.

**Friday 13**    "**£5,000 a Show.**" Tony Hancock, the BBC's top comedian is switching to ITV and will more than double his money.

**Saturday 14**    "**Weeping Liz Walks Out Alone.**" Elizabeth Taylor and Richard Burton, who say they are 'warm friends', had their first real quarrel in a Rome nightclub – and she left in tears.

**Sunday 15**    "**New Threat to Air Trips.**" In the week before the Easter holidays, more than 5,000 workers employed by state and private airlines have threatened to "work-to-rule" and ban overtime.

## HERE IN BRITAIN

### "Supermarket Ale – At Cut Prices"

Britain's biggest drive-in supermarket was granted an 'off-sale' drinks licence this week. The store is part of the £4m Tesco group, opened in Leicester four months ago.

The magistrates who granted the licence were told that because of Tesco's trading methods, the supermarket was able to cut overheads and pass on benefits to the customer. BUT, there would be no self-service for drinks, bottles will be sold from a special kiosk by trained staff.

After the hearing, a company spokesman said that the drinks most likely to be sold at cut prices were canned beers and some of the cheaper wines.

## AROUND THE WORLD

### "No TV In South Africa"

The luxury living whites of South Africa, centre of the world's gold and diamond industries, have almost all they can want in the way of material possessions. A typical middle-class worker can afford a four bedroom house, a spacious garden with possibly a swimming pool or tennis court, and a couple of African servants. But they have no television as it is banned by the Afrikaner Nationalist Government the main reason being, apartheid.

The introduction of TV would mean that the same entertainment was available for both black and white viewers – an altogether undesirable state of affairs as it might give Africans, "ideas above their station!"

# SHAMEFUL BRITISH CARS

*The Ford Classic 4-Door de Luxe*

Six more British cars are critically analysed after 12,000 miles running in the second "*Which!*" car supplement of the Consumers' Association. Most of them, in the 1½ litre £800 - £950 range, emerged from the tests better than the first group of cheaper cars dealt with in January. However, the report says, none was delivered in any better condition. Again, the testers are highly critical of defects that developed during running.

The cars tested were the Austin A60 Cambridge de Luxe, Ford Classic 4-door de Luxe, Ford Consul 315, Hillman Super Minx, Singer Vogue and Vauxhall Victor Super. Of these, the A60 and Classic are chosen as "joint best buys".

The Vogue says *Which?* was the most expensive at £100 more than the Super Minx but in performance had only a higher top speed. The Consul did not represent the same value for money as the other cars, the report states. The Super Minx developed "a large number of irritating and often serious faults," many the same as the Vogue, although many modifications have been made.

The Victor was easiest to service and to clean and look after generally, but had slightly worse acceleration, poor handbrake and some minor disadvantages and annoyances. The A60 had no major disadvantages, except an uncomfortable ride in the back and its performance was "average or better". The Classic was satisfactory. Very little went wrong with the A60 and not much with the Classic, Consul and Victor, the testers say, "But quite a lot went wrong with the Super Minx and the Vogue and both were delivered in a worse condition than the other cars.

The report says, "*An article for which the customer pays £550 - £650 before the addition of purchase tax really ought to have a clean bill of health in the mileage for which we run it – about a years' normal use … Nobody ought to have to pay £550 to be a guinea pig.*"

## IN THE NEWS

**Monday 16**    "**Crooks Cash-In Their Chips**" The hunt is on for a gang who are stealing tons of potatoes from Eire, smuggling them into Northern Ireland and then shipping them to England.

**Tuesday 17**    "**Extra Payment for Family Doctors.**" Health Minister Enoch Powell announced a £250,000 share out for doctors who keep up with the latest medical discoveries.

**Wednesday 18**    "**Deadlock Over EEC Treaty.**" The Dutch and Belgians have halted the talks for a European political union until Britain joins the Common Market.

**Thursday 19**    "**Burgess & Maclean.**" Scotland Yard issued arrest warrants after all-day rumours that the run-away Diplomats were on their way back to London from Russia. However, they did not show.

**Friday 20**    "**Good Friday.**" Ex General Salan, head of the French Secret Army [OAS] was arrested in Algiers and flown into Paris in chains.

**Saturday 21**    "**Eire Frees IRA Prisoners.**" All 29 Republican prisoners in the Republic of Ireland were released following the announcement of a border cease-fire in January and no incidents since then.

**Sunday 22**    "**Sizzling Easter Sunday.**" Temperatures rose to 63°F (17°C) in London, but were still 5°F (2°C) under the record for Easter Day, 1952.

## HERE IN BRITAIN

**"Mr Marples' New Safety Guide"**

"Don't lose your temper with other drivers – if you want to stay alive".

Mr Marples said, "When a young chap in a high-powered sports car passes you, don't show irritation. Even when someone else's behaviour makes irritation quite justified, put courtesy first and give the learner something good to imitate."

He also said:

• Drive defensively – that's the secret of road safety.

• Drive as if the other chap is a complete fool. Don't expect perfect behaviour!

"Two things are wanted on the road – responsibility and skill. All I can do is appeal for the first and perhaps punish those who do not show it."

## AROUND THE WORLD

**"Cuba To Free First Batch Of prisoners"**

The Cuban government this week agreed to release 54 Americans taken prisoner during the failed "Bay of Pigs" invasion by the CIA to oust Cuban leader Fidel Castro in April 1961. The men, all of them sick or wounded flew from Havana to Miami on Saturday.

In total there are 1,179 prisoners who were recently sentenced to up to 30 years' hard labour for their part in the invasion.

The Cuban government had put a ransom on each of them, promising that each would be released on payment of an amount which totalled $62m. [£22m] No details have been revealed, but it is understood that a sum of money was to be paid to the National Bank of Cuba before the 54 men would be released.

# BRITAIN'S BIGGEST PLANE

Britain's biggest airliner, the four jet Vickers VC10 was taken from its hangar in Weybridge, Surrey, for the first time yesterday and into view came the towering tailplane, high as a four-storey house, dominating the skyline.

Before it flies, the plane must complete a series of intensive pre-flight checks scheduled to last six weeks.

With a crowd of employees who watched the new aircraft rolled out of the hangar were Sir George Edwards, designer of the Viscount and now managing director of British Aircraft Corporation and Mr Jock Bryce and Mr Brian Trubshaw, the test pilots who will take the VC10 on its maiden flight.

The airliner weighs 150 tons fully loaded and is 158ft long. It will carry 150 passengers at 600mph over distances exceeding 4,000 miles.

Up to now 54 VC10s have been ordered. Deliveries to BOAC will begin at the end of 1963.

The British Aircraft Corporation embodies the aircraft and guided weapons resources of Bristol Aircraft, English Electric Aviation, Vickers-Armstrongs and Hunting Aircraft, each of which has its own distinguished record in the field of aeronautics.

# APRIL 23ᴿᴰ - 29ᵀᴴ 1962

## IN THE NEWS

**Monday 23**  "**Easter Scorcher Goes On**". Forecasters said that during the whole of Easter the holiday weather will be hot and sunny. The downside is that it will bring tens of thousands of families out on the roads, with cars streaming from the towns and cities to the countryside and coast.

**Tuesday 24**  "**Stirling Moss in Miracle Escape.**" Race Ace trapped for 40 minutes after crash at 120mph on the track at Goodwood yesterday. Moss lost consciousness and remained in a coma as he was taken to hospital.

**Wednesday 25**  "**Airports Facing Work to Rule Again.**" Some 5,000 supervisors and technicians will begin a "go-slow" on May 1ˢᵗ unless agreement is reached on their pay claim.

**Thursday 26**  "**£20m Whitbread Bid for Flowers.**" Whitbread & Co, the London brewery are making a bid for Flowers Breweries of Luton. Together they would control some 3,000 pubs.

**Friday 27**  "**First Anglo-American Rocket.**" Britain's first satellite, the UK 1 was launched at Cape Canaveral by an American Delta rocket. It carries equipment for studying cosmic radiation.

**Saturday 28**  "**Dock Strike Threat by 70,000.**" Unions vote for national shutdown on May 13ᵗʰ. The first to hit all the docks since the General Strike of 1926.

**Sunday 29**  "**De Gaulle and Elysee Palace Under Protection.**" It is believed that fanatical members of the OAS Secret Army have slipped into France from Algiers with orders to assassinate the President.

## HERE IN BRITAIN

**"Campaign For Nuclear Disarmament"**

Tens of thousands of people marched the 50 miles from the Atomic Weapons Research Establishment at Aldermaston, Berkshire, to London on the annual "Ban the Bomb" Easter march.

It ended this week at Hyde Park in London, with a rally watched by about 40,000 people.

The demonstration would have been held in Trafalgar Square as in previous years, but the Square had been "booked" for a rival "Keep Britain Great" rally attended by 500 people.

## AROUND THE WORLD

**"BBC Disc Jockeys
Banned From Picking 'Spins'"**

Song 'pluggers', the men who are paid by music publishers to get tunes played on the radio are often accused of being too 'cosy' with the disc jockeys. To stop this the BBC will provide DJs with a list of songs to play.

"Housewife's Choice" has 8,000,000 daily listeners who make thousands of song requests so now the disc jockeys will write their own linking material from the housewives' postcards but play the list the BBC producers supply.

# SEATTLE WORLD FAIR

*The 600ft High Space Needle Built For The Seattle 1962 World Fair*

President Kennedy opened the World's Fair at Seattle by remote control from Palm Beach, Florida, where he pressed a telegraph key which "bounced" a radio signal off a satellite orbiting the earth to the fairground, putting into action a carillon of more than 500 bells in the 600ft high 'space needle' which dominates the show.

he main theme of the fair, which is officially known as the Century 21 Exposition, is "man in the space age". While there is much to entertain and amuse the 10 million people expected to visit Seattle in the next six months, there is also emphasis on science, industry and technology.

The UK, which is among the dozen countries officially taking part in the fair, is represented by a pavilion covering a quarter of an acre, with a glazed and aluminium façade 150ft long, bearing an illuminated royal coat of arms. The introductory section of the pavilion is designed to show the adventurous spirit and ingenuity of the British people from the reign of Queen Elizabeth I, with a tableau portraying the two Elizabeths. A spoken commentary reminds visitors that Britain's modern adventurers seek new worlds to conquer, not on the high seas but in laboratories and research stations throughout Britain.

Throughout the expo, Britain features such projects as an advanced gas cooled reactor, a national programme for atomic power, revolutionary marine radar, research into ship design, blind landing for aircraft and the latest techniques in heart surgery. They promote the motor industry, agricultural machinery, shipbuilding and heavy electrical plant, aircraft and air navigation controls, machine tools and electronics.

# APRIL 30TH - MAY 6TH 1962

## IN THE NEWS

**Monday 30**      **"Nurses March in Pay Protest."** Thousands walked down Oxford Street behind a brass band, most wearing their navy blue cloaks with their scarlet hoods flung back and white caps.

**Tues 1st May**      **"Speed Limit Again at Weekends."** Better driving with fewer accidents on the 50mph restricted roads last summer, has led Mr Marples to impose the limit again this summer.

**Wednesday 2**      **"The Queen in Amsterdam."** Royal Celebrations and Festivities to begin for the silver wedding of Queen Juliana and Prince Bernhard of the Netherlands.

**Thursday 3**      **"Ford Walkout for the Nurses."** Ford workers at Dagenham agreed to a one-hour-walkout in protest at the 7d (3p) a day pay rise offer to nurses.

**Friday 4**      **"35,000 Miners to Support Nurses."** The pitmen, in Derbyshire, are prepared to walk out in sympathy with the nurses.

**Saturday 5**      **"East-West Hope of Points of Agreement."** The present tactical lull in the Soviet cold war campaign should encourage the west to search for areas of agreement, but without relaxing vigilance.

**Sunday 6**      **"Polaris Submarine Fires Nuclear Warhead."** This was the first to be exploded after being launched by a rocket in the test series in the Pacific.

## HERE IN BRITAIN

**"Millionaire Wins £38,000 On The Pools"**

**Lucky?**

He has a £50,000 house with an indoor, heated, swimming pool and a luxury yacht in the south of France.

The money will go to local charities, the winner knows what it is like to be hard up. He is the ninth of ten children, brought up in the East End and his first job was selling sacks of coal for 10s (50p) a week.

He spent 2 years saving the £20 to buy his first lorry and now has several businesses in the South East.

## AROUND THE WORLD

**"Drugs Found In Cruiser"**

A world-wide hunt started this week for a gang who tried to use HMS Belfast as a carrier for smuggling £2,000,000 worth of drugs, heroin and opium, and gems worth £25,000.

The contraband was seized mid-Pacific as the Belfast sailed from Singapore to San Francisco.

Two Chinese, a steward and canteen assistant were arrested and confined to cells until the ship arrives back in Plymouth. They are expected to stand trial for the illegal importation of banned substances.

# KING BREAKS FREE

*Dartmoor Prison Is High Up On Dartmoor At An Altitude Of 420m (1400ft)*

A Dartmoor prisoner, Albert King, wriggled and twisted his way out of the jail this week. He left behind one of the biggest escape puzzles in the prison's history. King, who was serving a twelve-year sentence for safe breaking, dug a hole in the floor of his cell and tunnelled a way to a ventilating shaft leading out to the prison yard.

He put a dummy in his bed to fool prison officers making the regular night check. Then, in his pants and vest and with his body apparently greased, he wriggled through the shaft. The next stage was to squeeze through a 14in by 10in grille into the yard. He emerged in the darkness of early morning. The next barrier was the 20ft high outer wall of the jail. Once over that, it is believed that he was picked up by a friend with clothes and a car.

King's getaway was in the pattern of escape which is regarded as a Dartmoor "classic" – that of "Rubber Bones Webb" in 1951 who also dug up his cell floor, left a dummy and wriggled out through a ventilation shaft. Like Webb, "Corkscrew" King left the jail authorities with some puzzling problems.

• How did he break open the stone floor of his cell without being seen or heard and how did he get rid of the rubble?
• How did he grease his body for the twist through the shaft?
• How did he climb the 20ft high wall? With a ladder like "Rubber Bones Webb"?

"Corkscrew King" is a determined escaper. This week's getaway was his third in six years. His father appealed to him *"Please give yourself up. Your Ma and I want you to earn maximum remission otherwise I may not live long enough to see you again!"*

# MAY 7TH - MAY 13TH 1962

## IN THE NEWS

**Monday 7**  "**Dakota Crashes in the Fog**." Ten holiday makers were hurt and another seven people on board the aircraft were injured, in the crash on St Boniface Down, Isle of Wight.

**Tuesday 8**  "**Soviet Subs Snoop on H-Tests.**" Soviet ships are keeping watch on America's nuclear tests of the Polaris rocket, held off Britain's Christmas Island in the Pacific.

**Wednesday 9**  "**Pay-Fight for Nurses Near Victory.**" In a climb-down by the Government, Cabinet Ministers have decided this is one pay battle they cannot win.

**Thursday 10**  "**Army Ready to Move**." Faced with a national Dock strike on Monday after peace talks failed, the Government will bring the troops in, if necessary, to maintain essential supplies and services.

**Friday 11**  "**Hopes of a British European Airways Settlement.**" After a month of industrial action following the suspension of 111 electricians over a 6d (2.5p) an hour pay claim.

**Saturday 12**  "**Dockers Reject Plan to Defer Strike.**" Mr George Woodcock, Secretary of the TUC said, "Before it takes place, there is some hope, but at the moment it is all "England to a China orange" we shall have a strike!"

**Sunday 13**  "**Dock Strike Called Off.**" Just 25 hours before the deadline, a 'pay and hours' agreement was made which dealt a staggering blow to Government policy.

## HERE IN BRITAIN

### "Output Of Royal Mint A Record"

Combining UK coins and coins minted for overseas governments, last year's output was 836,337,756 coins, the highest ever attained.

Coins were struck in 77 different denominations for 25 Commonwealth and foreign countries.

For Britain there were:
112m sixpences (2.5p),
26m half-crowns (12.5p) , 38m florins (20p),
43m shillings (5p), 41m threepenny bits (1p)
[half the previous year's total] and
40m pennies (0.5p).
But for the first year since 1860, not a single halfpenny (0.2p) left the coinage press.

## AROUND THE WORLD

### "Sympathetic Italians"

The Italians find much to be puzzled about in Britain, but the current shortage of potatoes has brought about a rare reaction of sympathy.

"The beloved dish," one Italian correspondent wrote, "has vanished from many a table". The news that "fish was served without chips" was seen as akin to "macaroni without cheese".

Wry comment was made that some in Britain advocated substituting spaghetti for potatoes during the shortage.

This from a people who had for so long made fun of the Italians for eating too much of it!

# TEN POUND POMS

*The SS Australis Transported Migrants From Britain To Australia*

During the past three months Australian immigration officials have been conducting an intensive recruiting campaign in the United Kingdom to entice skilled workers to Australia.

Australian officials interview possible emigrants in our employment exchanges where their advertisements are posted on the walls. Britain also makes a contribution, albeit not a very substantial one, to the assisted passage scheme. Our Government does not have the actual figures of how many skilled men emigrate but an analysis of the figures given by the receiving countries show that in the first six months of last year about 2,800 skilled men left the United Kingdom and Eire for Australia.

This year the Aussies ran a systematic campaign. In February they concentrated on the Midlands, the north-east and Scotland, in March on Lancashire, Yorkshire and Northern Ireland, and in April on London and the south and south-west. The list of skilled men they sought might well be a list of the craftsmen of which British manufacturers are most in need, from fitters and boilermakers, locksmiths to radio and television engineers.

Their advertisements draw a rosy picture of life for tradesmen in Australia. The passage costs only £10 from door to door for adults (hence the Ten Pound Pom) and an unlimited number of children under nineteen may travel free. There are "thousands of jobs for skilled workers" it is stated, particularly for metal and electrical tradesmen. They can "win the rich rewards of a new life in a naturally rich country. Nowhere in the world is the skill of the tradesman more appreciated or better rewarded."

There is a 40-hour, five-day week for all and average earnings are $A23 for men (just over £18). Taxes are lower. There is an average of five to eight hours sunshine a day. It is normal to own a car, and seven out of 10 Australians are buying their own home.

# MAY 14TH - 20TH 1962

## IN THE NEWS

**Monday 14**    "**US Marines Ready to Land in Siam**". Military intervention in Laos possible. Siam borders on Laos where Communist rebels have gained a series of victories in the past few days.

**Tuesday 15**    "**Wait and See**". A new pay offer to the nurses was made without the Minister saying 'how much' or over 'what period' but it would be more than the 6d (2.5p) in the pound government cap.

**Wednesday 16**    "**New Girl's Borstal in Bloom**" The plans for Bullwood Borstal include a sunlit courtyard filled with flowers and the windows surrounding it are barred with pale blue fret-work.

**Thursday 17**    "**Ex General Salan on Trial in Paris.**" But his French Secret Army terrorists continue the killing of locals in Algiers.

**Friday 18**    "**Load of Nails**" The driver of a lorry which spilt thousands of nails on the road causing 160 punctures and closing the road for 3 hours was fined £10 at Gloucester Court.

**Saturday 19**    "**Singapore and Malaya Merger.**" Prime Minister Mr Lee Quan Yew forecast that the countries would be in a Federal relationship by June 1963.

**Sunday 20**    "**Marilyn Monroe sings for President Kennedy.**" At a party last night, the Hollywood star sang a uniquely phrased rendering of 'Happy Birthday to You'.

## HERE IN BRITAIN

"Workers Calm The Storm In the Tea Urns".

When 350 tea-trolley girls at Fords walked out during the day over a 10s a week pay claim, it led to a dispute which cost £25,000 of production. Mid-morning the paint sprayers downed tools and demanded time to go to a local café for tea. Minutes later, hundreds more men also began nipping out for tea, taking longer than the official ten-minute break, until chaos on the production lines caused all work to stop and 5,000 men were sent home.

Fords called the dispute "the craziest ever" and appealed to the night-shift workers to bring their own tea and sandwiches! Which they did.

## AROUND THE WORLD

"81-Year-Old Leads Tunnel Escape In Berlin."

A group of 12 elderly East Germans escaped through a tunnel to West Berlin this week. In 16 days, they dug a tunnel 6ft high and 120ft long from the outskirts of the city to the French sector.

A first attempt to build the tunnel from beneath the house of the 81-year-old leader, had failed. So, he began to plant and replant little fir trees right under the noses of the communist border guards to find out where the ground was best suited for their purpose.

The men filled about 3,500 buckets with earth and carried them to a shed 80 yards away without detection.

# PANDAS REPLACE ZEBRAS

Panda crossings were introduced six weeks ago as a "new idea in pedestrian safety" and the 12 in Guildford have caused such bewilderment that a local newspaper this week called the experiment a farce.

Mechanical troubles have beset the pandas from the moment they were unveiled, and sackcloth has shrouded some of them here for as much as a week at a time while repairs were awaited. Until the middle of this week there had not been a day when one or another of the 12 had not been out of action.

Guildford was selected for the experiment because of the "high standard of intelligence" of its inhabitants, but this intelligence has been strained to the limit! Pedestrians are instructed to press a button which lights up a 'Wait' sign. An amber light flashing for five seconds should then warn drivers to stop. This should be followed by a pulsating red light for the driver and a 'Cross' sign for the pedestrian. Eight seconds later the red light should be replaced by flashing amber, the 'Cross' sign should start to flash, then both lights should go out so that drivers are free to proceed.

*"Looks like Blackpool front gone mad,"* commented one local taxi driver, and certainly, when the pandas are working smoothly they are difficult enough to master. But when they have been out of action the question has been, who has the right of way? Does a panda which is not working become a zebra? Everyone here has his own theory and pedestrians and motorists have put different theories into practice on the same crossing at the same time with hair raising results.

# MAY 21ST - 27TH 1962

## IN THE NEWS

**Monday 21**     "**Handmaids to do School Chores**". The Minister of Education agreed that qualified teachers in primary schools would have more teaching time if a "handmaid" took over minding the children.

**Tuesday 22**     "**Plot to Kill De Gaulle.**" A plot to assassinate the President over the weekend was foiled and 16 "terrorists" of the OAS in Algiers have been arrested.

**Wednesday 23** "**West End Musicians to go on Strike.**" Members of the theatre orchestras will 'down instruments' in their fight for more money.

**Thursday 24**     "**Salan Escapes the Guillotine.**" The self-confessed leader of the French terrorist Secret Army (OAS) is sentenced to life imprisonment.

**Friday 25**     "**Dramatic End to US Space Flight.**" An astronaut orbited the earth three times before losing contact for 45 minutes. He was picked up 3 hours later in the Atlantic, 200 miles from the intended position.

**Saturday 26**     "**Soviet Ships Monitoring US Tests Again.**" Their ships cruising near Christmas Island are gathering valuable military information.

**Sunday 27**     "**No Milk Today Thank You!**" More than 200,000 homes in the Midlands will not have their milk delivery today as the Roundsmen are on strike.

## HERE IN BRITAIN

### "Car With Aluminium Bumpers."

This week a new car was announced – the Triumph Vitesse and it will be setting the trend. It has extruded aluminium bumpers, the world's first on a production car.

They are only half the weight of steel, yet as strong and more resilient. They will not rust or peel and can withstand greater impact shocks without permanent damage.

Another bonus, the brilliant finish is an integral part of the metal and not a superficial plating and for the designer, the extrusion process provides a greater freedom in styling.

## AROUND THE WORLD

### "Hottest May Day On Record In New York"

The temperature in New York rose to 99F (37C) one day this week making it the hottest of any day in May in the weather bureau's 94 years of record keeping.

At its peak, reached in mid-afternoon, the temperature was only a few deg. below the highest ever experienced in the city, 102.3F (39C) on July 9, 1936.

Among those suffering in the heat were 10,000 soldiers, sailors, marines and airmen in full battle dress and cadets from Westpoint Military Academy, who paraded on Fifth Avenue in celebration of Armed Forces Day.

# COVENTRY CATHEDRAL

*The Old (right) And New (left) Cathedral Buildings. After The Bombing (Inset)*

The Consecration of the new Cathedral Church of St. Michael was a ceremony of "simple yet luxurious beauty" in the presence of the Queen and performed by the Bishop of Coventry.

It was the culmination of seven years of work and the fulfilment of more than twenty years of faith and hope that the old building destroyed during the last war, would rise again, and was witnessed by a congregation of nearly 2,000 who occupied every available place in the new building and a stand erected among the ruins of the old.

Just after 2pm the eleven processions of archbishops, bishops and clergy with civic leaders began to enter the cathedral and they took nearly an hour to file through the glass west door. Last but one came the Queen's procession, preceded by her Gentlemen-at-Arms, their white plumes supplying the occasion with a sort of instant awe. This included Princess Margaret, Lord Snowdon and Sir Basil Spence – the architect of the new Cathedral.

Earlier in the week, the very first service to be held in the completed cathedral took place for a thousand men and women whose "hands raised the £1,500,000 building from the blitzed ashes of the war."

Some 'hands' spent 30,000 hours of work on the tapestry which is the cathedral's crowning glory. The Provost told them, "*This service is to honour you, the craftsmen, the skilled men, the labourers, the typists and all the backroom boys and girls. This is your day.*"

# MAY 28ᵗʰ - JUNE 3ᴿᴰ 1962

## IN THE NEWS

**Monday 28**    **"West Accused Over Berlin Wall Explosions."** Three explosions occurred on the eastern side between the French and Soviet sectors during the early hours of the morning.

**Tuesday 29**    **"Ford Reject Pay Claim by 45,000".** The Ford Motor Company refused any increase in wages because of 'anxiety on their profit position'.

**Wednesday 30**    **"Share Prices Slide."** Lowest since 1959. Prices were slashed on the Stock Exchange yesterday in the sharpest reaction for a generation. This was in response to an overnight slump on Wall Street.

**Thursday 31**    **"New Warning on Meat Price."** Shopping bills may go up as wholesale prices at Smithfield Market have shot up 15-20%.

**Friday 1ˢᵗ June**    **"Eichmann Dies Unrepentant."** Found guilty in Nurenburg of killing 6m Jews he was hanged in Tel Aviv, cremated on a police boat and his ashes scattered at sea.

**Saturday 2**    **"Going For A Song"** Tyneside starts a week of celebrations to mark the centenary of the song, "Blaydon Races". £20,000 has been spent on 350 flower baskets, two and a half miles of bunting and 2,000 pennants.

**Sunday 3**    **"Car Workers Revolt."** The workers say "strike crazy shop stewards" who are continuously paralysing the motor industry, "must go."

## HERE IN BRITAIN

### "Frank Sinatra Strolls Around London"

Frank Sinatra walked unnoticed around the West End on Wednesday. Without his trade mark hat, wearing flannels and a blazer, hardly anyone recognised him.

The American singer flew into London, by private plane from Madrid, two days before he was expected. He is here to give the first of his British charity concerts at the Festival Hall, part of his world charity tour.

The badge on his blue blazer has the letters J.D., standing for Jack Daniels; a square whisky bottle, four golf clubs and six golf balls. He wears it to show he plays golf as well as drinks whisky!

## AROUND THE WORLD

### "Warning To The Service Men In Gibraltar."

This week the Royal Air Force and Army authorities began a drive to stamp out smuggling after a third British Serviceman has been caught trying to smuggle goods from Gibraltar to neighbouring Spain.

The RAF Station Commander has issued an order telling his men: "If you are caught smuggling – you are on your own. The RAF will not help you and if convicted by a Spanish court, you may be kicked out of the Service."

The order also warns that if there are any more cases, all airmen may be forbidden to visit Spain. Two of the three Servicemen caught this month, are now serving time in Spanish jails.

# COSTLY CHIPS IN BRIGHTON

Fanfares sounded, footmen in perfect uniforms stood to attention as Britain's first casino opened its doors this week. Lords and Ladies, businessmen, jockeys, race-horse trainers, lawyers and some east-end boys who'd done well, filed into the palatial Regency styled Clarence Room of the Metropole Hotel to chance their luck. Three massive £5,000 chandeliers were suspended from a domed roof where 60,000 crystals burst into light as the guests queued at the £150,000 "bank" to change their cash or cheques into "chips". The smallest chip was worth 2s 6d (12.5p) but there was also a £1,000 chip, crimson and beautifully decorated. The Casino boasts a "walk-in safe."

Membership is three guineas (£3.15) a year or you can pay by the quarter, one guinea (£1.05) a time and the minimum stake at most tables is £1 – but when you take your seat, you are charged a fee ranging from 2s 6d (12.5p) to £50, depending on your table. This will cover 45 minutes of play, so six hours in a "High Stakes Room" could mean £400 before placing a single bet! Under the British gambling laws, casinos are not allowed to take a percentage of the takings – only these fees - and at Brighton there are a staff of one hundred to pay!

On offer are, chemin de fer, dice, roulette, poker and kaluki (a form of rummy). Rivalling Monte Carlo for its splendour, Brighton casino is not for those who want a half-crown flutter. One East Ender in evening dress was overheard to say, "Blimey, I thought I could enjoy myself on a pony (£25) but that's not going to anywhere in this dive."

The Metropole has a distinguished career, built in 1890 at a cost of £57,000, on its opening, 1500 people arrived on a special train from London. On the 14th November 1896 the front of the hotel was the finishing post for the first London to Brighton car run. The cars left from the London Metropole, and the event is still held every year to celebrate the abolishment of the speed limit.

# JUNE 4TH - 10TH 1962

## IN THE NEWS

**Monday 4**   "**130 Killed in Airliner Crash at Paris.**" An Air France Boeing 707 on a flight to Atlanta, crashed after take-off from Orly Airport, Paris,in the worst recorded air disaster involving a single aircraft.

**Tuesday 5**   "**Macmillan Back From "Very Cordial" Common Market Talks.**" The emphasis was on Anglo-French 'Community of Interest' in his talks with President De Gaulle.

**Wednesday 6**   "**It's Derby Day.**" It's anyone's guess who will come first past the post – "it's, pick it with a pin", and the weather is fine too.

**Thursday 7**   "**Seven Horses Fall in the Derby.**" Six jockeys were taken to hospital and one horse, King Canute II,was destroyed, in a race that resembled the Grand National.

**Friday 8**   "**Queen Mother in Canada.**" As Commander in Chief, Queen Elizabeth the Queen Mother arrived in Montreal to attend the centenary celebrations of the Black Watch Regiment of Canada.

**Saturday 9**   "**What a Beautiful Whitsun Weekend.**" The forecast is for a record breaking 'scorcher'. The rush to get out of town to the sea is already under way by road, rail and air.

**Sunday 10**   "**70 Miles of Traffic Jams**". With hundreds of thousands of motorists on the move, the AA called it "a Sunday Spectacular".

## HERE IN BRITAIN

### "Please Don't Come To Coventry Cathedral"

The new Coventry Cathedral is swamped every day by thousands of tourists.

The Provost complained of sightseers just too numerous to control. In one incident, a church steward was punched in the chest and knocked down as he tried to usher out tourists before a church service.

Some people queuing for an hour to get in are openly angry if we have to turn them away because a service is about to start. "We recognise and welcome the interest in our wonderful new building, but we must put its function as a place of worship first."

## AROUND THE WORLD

### "Who's For Canaveral?"

A competition being run in "The Daily Mirror" offered any boy or girl between 12 and 18 the chance to win "Project Space", a fabulous eight-day, 10,000 mile trip to the New World. The winners will fly to Florida and on to the Cape Canaveral Space station.

To win, they had to reply to the imaginary job advert "WANTED: SPACEMEN AND SPACEWOMEN." by writing in no more than 100 words why they would like it and why they would be suitable. Four winners were chosen for this fabulous trip by "The Mirror", four more from competitions in the "Look and Learn", and "The Eagle" comics and two chosen from the visitors to the Boys and Girls Exhibition in London this summer.

# DUKE WARNS OF EXTINCTION

The Duke of Edinburgh was in New York for the inaugural dinner of the US branch of the World Wildlife Fund and warned his audience that our descendants could be forced to live in a world where the only living creature would be man himself – *"always assuming, of course,"* he said, *"that we don't destroy ourselves as well in the meantime."*

The World Wildlife Fund was set up in September last year, with its headquarters in Zurich, to raise money for the preservation of wildlife and wild places. So far, the fund has given money to more than 20 projects designed to preserve rare species of wildlife. They include an attempt to save the last white rhino in Uganda, the whooping crane, which breeds in Canada, the purchase of land in Tanganyika which will help to protect the Ngurdoto Crater National Park; and measures for preserving the orang-utang in Borneo.

In his speech, the Duke described the poachers who were threatening the extermination of many big game animals in Africa as "killers for profit … the get-rich-at-any-price mob." African poachers, he said, were killing off the rhinoceros to get its horn for export to China, "where, for some incomprehensible reason, they seem to think it acts as an aphrodisiac."

The Duke also criticized the status seekers – people "like the eagle chasers". The bald eagle in North America was being chased and killed by people in light aeroplanes who seem to think it smart to own its feathers and claws.

*"What is needed, above all now,"* he said, *"are people all over the world who understand the problem and really care about it. People who have the courage to see that the conservation laws are obeyed."*

# JUNE 11ᵀᴴ – 17ᵀᴴ 1962

## IN THE NEWS

**Monday 11**   **"52 British Soldiers Face Court Martial."** Following drunken brawls, this is the largest number of charges the British Army of the Rhine has ever faced in a single month.

**Tuesday 12**   **"Peace for Laos."** The nine years civil war in Laos, which could have become the starting point of a new world conflict, ends today with the three feuding princes signing a coalition agreement.

**Wednesday 13**   **"Nurses Turn Down Pay Offer."** Hopes of ending the ten-month-old pay battle slumped when a new round of bargaining failed to break the deadlock.

**Thursday 14**   **"Sweets Peril on a Dump."** Tons of sweets and chocolates, written off after a factory fire, were found by children on a council tip in Lancashire. But the authorities soon stepped in, warning they were dangerous.

**Friday 15**   **"Police Fired on in Bank Raid."** A gunman held a woman hostage in a bank raid in Liverpool and when he fled with £1,000 in £5 notes, shot at the chasing police.

**Saturday 16**   **"Paris Expects OAS leader to Face New Trial."** French terrorist chief, Raoul Salan, who escaped the guillotine last month may face new charges and another death penalty.

**Sunday 17**   **"Man Accused of Knifing MP."** Sir Walter Bromley-Davenport was stabbed in the courtyard of his home in Cheshire by a man who told him, "You have no right to a title, no-one should have a title."

## HERE IN BRITAIN

### "So Where Was that Whit Sun?"

A Tory MP attacked the weathermen on Tuesday over the Whit Monday sun-that-never-was. After listening carefully to the forecast when the Met men had predicted sunshine for his area, he went sailing from his country home in Blakeney, Norfolk.

When no sunny periods or bright intervals broke through the rain, he called it, "A pretty disgraceful forecast," and added, "I may raise this in the House."

Earlier this year the MP had questioned the Air Minister about two wrong forecasts!

## AROUND THE WORLD

### "US Plans a Space Commando."

A leaked report has stated that President Kennedy has decided on a big policy switch and told his military leaders that "We must be prepared." He envisages a "Commando in Space" – a man in a satellite who could, if needed, destroy a hostile Spacecraft.

This Space Patrol would be entirely defensive and would aim only at preventing Russia from gaining "military control" of space. After the report of this project was published, the US Defence Department denied they were going to put military "teeth" into the civilian run Space programme but it is regarded as an "official leak" of a major policy change.

# POISON DWARFS

*The Main Square In Minden*

This week the British Army of the Rhine revealed that twenty-one soldiers serving in the Cameronians in Minden, Germany had been sentenced to detention by Army courts. Nineteen of the twenty-one were sentenced for their part in the "Battle of Minden Street" – a drunken café brawl.

The Germans plunged into the battle of words over the conduct of the British troops who committed 146 criminal offences in the town in the last year alone. An ex-wrestler, who owns the late-night Café Colosseum, where a recent battle led to detention for nineteen Scots, declared they had earned the nickname "Poison Dwarfs" because of the way their smallest soldiers kept getting into brawls and the Cameronians had the worst record.

He went on to say that he had asked that his bar was put out of bounds for the Scots, but the Army said if it was out of bounds for the Scots, it would have to be out of bounds for the English too." He then said, "the ENGLISH are ALL RIGHT!"

The men of the Cameronians answered back, angry at the charge and their nickname. One Glaswegian corporal said, "*The Germans think they are big – but it's only their heads that are big.*" A private added, "*What would you do if you were sworn at, then spat on? I tell you what we do – we hit 'em.*" The Cameronians loathe Minden, "*They won't let us into the dances and only the really rough pubs will serve us.*" A senior officer expressed the view that cheap drink was a principal cause of the recent incidents.

Claims that the British soldiers and their wives had been "insulted" by the Germans was refuted by a police official who said, "*There is not a word of truth in these reports as far as Minden is concerned. On the whole,*" he said, "*relations are cordial.*"

# JUNE 18TH - 24TH 1962

## IN THE NEWS

**Monday 18**    "**Algeria, It's all Over.**" The OAS – French Secret Army orders "End the bloodshed" after seven and a half years of fighting.

**Tuesday 19**    "**National Union of Railwaymen - Rail Closure Campaign.**" The NUR launched a nationwide campaign against the proposed economies. An initial government report identified 2,363 stations and 5,000 miles (8,000 km) of railway line for closure, which represents 55% of stations and 30% of route miles, plus the loss of 67,700 jobs.

**Wednesday 20**    "**OAS Shatter the Truce in Algeria.**" They made a murderous attack on a huge petrol dump in Oran, but the situation remained calm in the capital, Algiers.

**Thursday 21**    "**Licensed Clubs Go Dry**". A hundred establishments in Birmingham forgot the change in last year's Licensing Act which called for them to renew their alcohol licenses.

**Friday 22**    "**Stirling Moss to leave hospital today.**" The racing ace suffered severe injuries to his head, knee and shoulder in the 120mph crash at Goodwood on Easter Monday.

**Saturday 23**    "**110 Killed in Jet Crash.**" An Air France Boeing 707, on a flight from Paris to Chile, crashed in a raging thunderstorm on the island of Guadeloupe in the West Indies.

**Sunday 24**    "**More Havoc by British Troops.**" Ordered out of a public house in Schneverdingen, drunken and rowdy troops from the British Army of the Rhine (BAOR) went through the town breaking shop windows, damaging park benches, streetlamps and cars.

## HERE IN BRITAIN

### "Too Much Sex On Front Page."

The Archbishop of York said this week that too often, the sex life of some young woman made front page news in Britain's newspapers and that what made journalism a difficult profession was that the writer had to handle three things – truth, words and men.

"It has been said that a country gets the government that it deserves," he went on, "perhaps it is also true that it gets the journalism that it deserves, and that a corrupt society which glories in the salacious and the dirty will get the dirty press it deserves."

## AROUND THE WORLD

### "2,000 Riot Over The Price Of Artichokes."

Nearly 2,000 farmers rioted this week because they cannot get what they think is a fair price for artichokes. Scores of steel-helmeted police hurled tear-gas grenades into the mob in the Brittany town of St Pol de Leon.

The rioters – members of a collective farmers association – dumped tons of artichokes in the main streets of the town to immobilise traffic.

Then they attacked a Paris bound train carrying 500 crates of artichokes from independent growers. Fights broke out as the farmers smashed open crates and poured petrol over the vegetables.

# ADVERTS STUBBED OUT

Agreement was reached between the Independent Television Authority and representatives of tobacco manufacturers to exclude certain kinds of cigarette advertisements from commercial television broadcasts. In future such advertisements will be tested by the authority against an agreed set of rules.

The new rules will affect commercials that suggest you are not "in the swim socially" unless you smoke. The criteria to be observed will include advertisements which suggest that cigarette smoking is inseparable from masculinity – "the he-man happily inhaling on a cigarette". That it is a desirable recreation for young people – "boy meets girl", that it is a socially acceptable habit, that smoking produces ecstatic pleasure and that smoking is enjoyed by popular heroes or heroines.

With these rules in mind, it can be taken that advertising agencies with cigarette accounts are now working on new schemes that avoid such pitfalls. The likelihood is that future advertisements will tend to dwell, bearing in mind the fairly strict limitations involved, on praising the product's flavour, individuality and excellence.

The additional scrutiny to which cigarette advertisements will now be subjected was devised with the full cooperation of the tobacco manufacturers, who are said to have shown a full sense of importance of the question. The existence of the code will make it easier in some ways for the advertising industry to deal with their subject.

One advertiser said yesterday: "It *may be better to have some restrictions to work within rather than to have people sniping at you all the time and not to know whether you are right or wrong.*"

# JUNE 25TH - JULY 1ST 1962

## IN THE NEWS

**Monday 25**    "**Wimbledon Starts Today.**" The two thorny questions, are many players "shamateurs" (do they take money despite being amateur) and should women wear "all white"? Traditionalists fear that the game is coming under threat from top players being offered secret deals to promote tennis equipment.

**Tuesday 26**    "**Fires Wreck City.**" Terrorists blow up oil and petrol storage tanks, spreading fire through Oran, second city of Algeria, already burned by the OAS.

**Wednesday 27**    "**That's Wimbledon.**" Australia's No 1 seed, Margaret Smith was defeated by American college girl, Billie Jean Moffitt in a sensational first round.

**Thursday 28**    "**£190,000 Paid for a Rembrandt.**" What is thought to be the last Rembrandt of the 1660's, a portrayal of St Bartholomew, is to stay in Britain.

**Friday 29**    "**Sir Winston Churchill to Fly Back today by RAF Comet.**" Sir Winston (87) broke his thigh whilst on holiday in Monte Carlo.

**Saturday 30**    "**Maiden Flight by VC 10**". No engineering snags were found during the 19-minute journey of Britain's most powerful long range aircraft.

**Sun 1st July**    "**Fury at a Fascist Rally.**" Leaders of the Nationalist Socialist Movement were bombarded with rotten eggs and tomatoes at an anti-Jewish rally in Trafalgar Square.

## HERE IN BRITAIN

### "Tennis Star's Words Stop Big Match"

Australian tennis star Bob Hewitt caused a Wimbledon sensation when his match was stopped and the official referee called to the court. Hewitt had broken all Wimbledon etiquette by exploding into a sequence of hot words in the middle of his game with Denmark's Jorgen Ulrich.

Crowds gasped at one stage as Hewitt glaring shouted, "Bloody Fool." No one was sure for whom the words were intended – but the umpire believed they were for him.

More words flowed as Hewitt challenged line decisions and the umpire sent for the referee who said afterwards that Hewitt "had made veiled, if not audible, reference to his ancestry."

## AROUND THE WORLD

### "Monks Acquitted Of Extortion"

Four monks were this week acquitted on charges of taking part in a Mafia-type extortion system in central Sicily.

Three Sicilian peasants were sentenced to 30 years and a twenty year old "the boy bandit " jailed for 14 years. All had been charged with the murder of a landowner after refusing to pay extortion demands.

Witnesses told the court of a "reign of terror" at Mazzarino, where there is a monastery. The monks admitted that they passed on extortion demands and collected money for unknown persons, but they said they acted under duress, choosing a lesser evil to save their own lives and those of the intended victims.

# WINSTON BREAKS A LEG

*Sir Winston Churchill Broke His Leg Whilst Staying in Monaco*

This week Sir Winston Churchill (87) was in Monaco for his annual Riviera holiday but was found by his valet, after breakfast, lying in pain beside his bed in his hotel suite having slipped and broken his left thigh.  He was taken to the Princess Grace Hospital in Monte Carlo where an operation was carried out, under anaesthetic, to set the bone.

The doctors treating Sir Winston, described his resistance as "remarkable - positively Churchillian", and later in the evening, he asked for some cold chicken and brandy and was given both and seemed to enjoy them.

He was flown back to England the next day where Lady Churchill and Lord Moran had been waiting at the airport . As soon as the cabin door was open Lady Churchill, hat-less and wearing dark glasses, hurried up the steps with Lord Moran. A brief handshake with senior RAF medical officers who attended Sir Winston during the flight, and then forward to the specially equipped cabin where Sir Winston lay on a stretcher immediately behind the flight deck.

On the other side of the aircraft the door of the forward cabin was opened, and a fork-lift truck driven into position. Medical orderlies stepped on to the truck platform and eased the stretcher through the doorway. In the background a group of onlookers clapped and waved as the head of Sir Winston came into view. Glancing up at members of the Comet crew standing in the doorway high above him, Sir Winston gave a brief grin and raised his right hand to give them the V sign-perhaps a grateful acknowledgement of a smooth trip. Seconds later the sign was repeated as he was lifted into the ambulance.

## IN THE NEWS

**Monday 2** — **"Runaway Spy in Suicide Bid."** Robert Soblen, sentenced to life imprisonment in America for spying for Russia, slashed his wrists on the deportation flight to the US via London.

**Tuesday 3** — **"Algiers: Face to Face with Civil War."** Moslem factions were massing only a few hours after the referendum which gave the country independence from French rule.

**Wednesday 4** — **"3% In the Engineers' Pay Packets."** With no cuts in hours worked, this is another blow to the Tories pay policy of a 2 ½% "guiding light" for pay increases.

**Thursday 5** — **"A Second Channel for ITV".** Independent television as well as the BBC is to get a second channel and the Cabinet go ahead may be given within two months.

**Friday 6** — **"How to Beat Boredom on the Rhine."** War Minister says more English TV programmes and pubs on the bases will be provided to make soldiers feel more at home in Germany.

**Saturday 7** — **"Wimbledon Queue Camps Out."** More than 200 people were queuing at midnight for tickets for today's centre-court women's singles final between Karen Susman and Věra Sukova

**Sunday 8** — **"Sir Winston Churchill Sleeps Well."** Today there is no extension to yesterday's report of early signs of phlebitis [inflammation of the veins] in Sir Winston's injured left thigh and he was in good spirits.

### HERE IN BRITAIN

#### "A Bullfight Trip Rapped"

A Vicar yesterday attacked a Nottingham school's holiday party's visit to a Spanish bullfight. "Is it right that children should be allowed to see something that is not permitted in England?"

Parents had been told of the possibility of a bullfight visit and there had been no objections. A farmer whose son was on the trip said, "Going to a bullfight doesn't make them depraved children and it's something they will never have a chance to see again in their lives.

It's just a custom of the country no matter how long it's been banned over here and, as far as my boy was concerned, he didn't lose any sleep over it."

### AROUND THE WORLD

#### "Arab "Godiva" Rides In"

An unveiled, henna-haired Arab, "Lady Godiva" – wearing a bright green blouse and skirt – rode into the European quarter of Algiers this week, astride a gleaming white charger.

Her dramatic appearance in the colours of newly independent Algeria sent thousands of Moslem demonstrators into a frenzy, screaming triumphantly, "Algeria is ours." They streamed into the heart of the European quarter where frightened French people stayed huddled indoors behind closed shutters.

Millions of Moslems gave a massive "yes" to Algerian independence in the referendum held earlier this week after 132 years of French rule.

# BOY POISONS THREE

**POISON PERIL**
IN YOUR HOME

what to do about it right now

Poisons had become an obsession with a schoolboy, aged 14, and knowledge of their properties and effects gave him a sense of power, a doctor said at the Central Criminal Court this week. The London boy, Graham Young, had pleaded guilty to three charges of administering poisons to his father, his sister and his school friend so as thereby to cause them grievous bodily harm.

In May this year police went to the boy's school and found a handbook on poisons. At his home they recovered two books, one entitled "A poisoner in the dock" and the other, "Sixty famous trials." When questioned by the police the boy denied that he was then in possession of any poisons, but two bottles of thallium were found on him. At the police station the boy made a statement in which he said: "*I have been interested in poisons, their properties and effects since I was about 11.*" After describing how he bought various poisons, he said: " *I tried out one of them on my friend. I gave him two or three grains at school. I cannot remember how I caused him to take it. I think it was probably on a cream biscuit or a cake. He was sick after taking it. Later I gave him other doses. always on food.*"

*"After that I started experimenting at home by putting sometimes one and sometimes three grains of poison on prepared foods which my mother, father and sister would eat. Afterwards all my family was sick. By September of last year this had become an obsession with me and I continued to give members of my family small doses of antimony tartrate. One morning at the end of November I was getting ready to go to school when I saw my sister's cup of tea on the dresser. I put one-tenth of a grain of belladonna in the milk. That night my mother told me my sister had been ill during the day. She told me what the symptoms were, and I knew it was the effects of the belladonna".*

## IN THE NEWS

**Monday 9**     **"Mr Foulkes Sacked by ETU."** The Communist leader of the Electrical Trades Union for seventeen years, was expelled for bringing discredit on the Union.

**Tuesday 10**     **"One Mighty Flash Lights Up an Ocean."** America exploded in space their first Hydrogen bomb – The Rainbow Bomb - and lit up a vast area of the Pacific Ocean.

**Wednesday 11**    **"TV From Space"** A picture of a man's face was transmitted on British television screens from Telstar, the communications satellite, at exactly 1 am today and lasted for about two minutes.

**Thursday 12**     **"£400,000 Paintings Stolen."** Thirty-five French impressionist paintings were stolen from an art gallery in Carlos Place, Mayfair just hours before thieves tried to grab a Rembrandt from the Dulwich Art Gallery.

**Friday 13**     **"Bertrand Russell Backs Moscow March."** The head of the anti-nuclear 'Committee of 100', urged his followers to go ahead with a ban-the-bomb march in Moscow.

**Saturday 14**     **"Macmillan's Panic Purge."** Last night, the ageing premier sacked seven of his Ministers in a desperate bid to win back runaway Tory voters.

**Sunday 15**     **"New Blue Bird Held Down to 60mph."** 5,000 spectators watched Mr Donald Campbell carefully demonstrate the potentially fastest car in the world, at Goodwood.

## HERE IN BRITAIN
### "Bee Sting Plot To Snatch £30,000"

A plot to steal £30,000 from a train with the help of a swarm of bees has been foiled. The gang planned to release the bees to throw guards into a panic, then snatch mailbags containing the money.

The raid was organised by an attractive blonde. After a tip off about the pan the police named it "Operation bee sting". The gang learned that they would walk into an ambush – so they called it off.

A hunt has also been going on for three men said to be working for the blonde who is believed to be well educated and to have lived in the Kensington area for the past two years from where she frequents West End clubs and is noted for throwing lavish champagne parties.

## AROUND THE WORLD
### "Hard Work Drives German Recovery"

After the war their productive capacity was sufficient only to provide each German with:
ONE china plate every five years:
ONE pair of shoes once every twelve years:
ONE suit every fifty years:
Nappies for only one baby in five, and
ONE Coffin for every third German.

In ten years, they have
- Doubled factory output
- Increased exports four-fold
- Toppled Britain from her position as the world's second greatest exporting nation
- Boosted wages two and a half times
- Amassed gold reserves of £1,100m and
- Created a higher value for the Deutsch Mark against other world currencies.

# MASSIVE ART THEFT

*Painting By Cezanne*

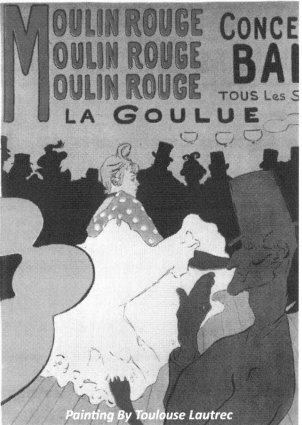

*Painting By Toulouse Lautrec*

"*I did not imagine anyone could get in that way.*" This addition to the list of famous last words was made by Mr O'Hana as he pointed out the way thieves entered his art gallery in Carlos Place, Mayfair, London to steal thirty five paintings worth £400,000 on the open market. Asked if there were any alarm systems protecting it he said, "*No, but this place is like a little fortress.*"

So it appeared until the night before last. The gallery has two exhibition rooms separated by a small courtyard. Usually, entrance is from the street by a heavy wrought-iron door, backed with glass, which can be firmly secured but the door from the courtyard which is the only entrance to the inner room is quite ordinary and it was to this that the thieves came. Mr. O'Hana said, "*They found the only possible way.*"

Paintings stolen include 12 Renoirs and others by Braque, Cezanne, Manet, Picasso, Sisley, Toulouse-Lautrec, Utrillo and Vuillard. "*How can anybody reappear with any of these? They are known the world over.*"

The raid on the O'Hana Gallery is thought to be the richest made in London and to bring the value of paintings stolen throughout the world during the past year to about £2,500,000.

Mr. O'Hana said that apart from minor pilfering he had lost nothing from his gallery until the previous night's disaster. Ruefully mentioning "stable doors and bolted horses" he said that probably he would have installed at the courtyard entrances, heavy iron doors similar to that at the street entrance

# JULY 16ᵀᴴ - 22ⁿᴰ 1962

## IN THE NEWS

**Monday 16**     **"Mac to Make Room for Bright Young Tories."** With plans to sack more Ministers this week, Mr Macmillan will try to promote from the junior ranks.

**Tuesday 17**     **"The Rumble of Revolt."** The great purge is over, but Mac's Conservative Party is dismayed and divided with a possible leadership battle to come.

**Wednesday 18**     **"Hovercraft for the Thames."** The new 'D2' Hovercraft is due on the Thames next week with the aim of starting a regular service between the Festival Hall and Pool of London.

**Thursday 19**     **"Doctors' New Plan."** In the wake of the thalidomide disaster, British doctors will be asked today to back a plan for the independent testing of ALL new drugs before they can be prescribed.

**Friday 20**     **"Anti-Missile Success for Missile."** A US missile intercepted a target travelling 4,500 miles away, at the same speed and course an incoming ballistic missile would travel.

**Saturday 21**     **"Maudling Gets a Warning."** Mr Reginald Maudling, the new Chancellor, was warned by top industrialists to give Britain's sagging economy a boost by cutting business taxes.

**Sunday 22**     **"British Cars' Grand Slam in Grand Prix."** It was Jim Clark all the way to the chequered flag in his new Lotus 25 as well as British cars in the first six places in yesterday's British GP at Aintree. John Surtees was second and Bruce McLaren third.

## HERE IN BRITAIN

### "Milk Delivered Very Slowly"

New rules were agreed for pedestrian controlled vehicles such as lawn mowers, when a lad called David Crane, with only a provisional licence, who had been earning his living pulling a milk float on his round for nine months, failed his test as he could not read a number plate at 25 yards.

The milk firm had to employ another man to pull the float while Crane walked alongside at the same pace. It had come as a shock to people in Blackburn to find how stupid the law could be. The maximum speed of the float when loaded was three and three-quarter miles an hour.

## AROUND THE WORLD

### "US Picks Up Our Colour TV"

British scientists made another big break-through in space-age communications this week. Colour television pictures were transmitted to outer space for the first time and received back *sharp and clear*. The transmission was made from Goonhilly Down in Cornwall to the satellite Telstar and back to the transmitting station.

But, the pictures were also picked up in Maine in the USA. A member of the Goonhilly team said, "The experiment has been a complete success, the pictures were received back here without any apparent loss of colour definition. Colour tests to the USA were scheduled for a future orbit so we are more than delighted."

The freezer cabinets of 100,000 shops will this year pull in £66m, twenty times more than only 10 years ago. Cleethorpes and Grimsby, once the heart of the UK fishing industry has become the world's most concentrated centre of the frozen food industry.

The quick success is attributed to the scientist Clarence Birdseye who realised during an Arctic hunting trip in the 1920s, that the Eskimo's food, preserved in natural ice, was frequently more palatable than that stored by domestic refrigerators. In the USA frozen foods now account for 5 per cent of the food budget.

In Britain, where the domestic freezer is still a comparative luxury, sales rose by more than 500% between 1955 and 1960. Some 700m fish fingers are among the 60,000 tons of frozen fish consumed and peas from 35,000 acres will be found on the same plates as 120,000 quick-frozen chickens.

In farming, the once-humble, pea now ranks in importance with wheat. The farmer signs a contract with firms like Bird's Eye and plants what they want, when they want and harvest it when told to by the company. For example, Unilever say they tested 300 types of green bean before a stringless variety which grows to within two feet of the ground, exactly fitting the feeder forks of a mobile harvester, was decided on.

The farmer will also be told what insecticides to use and when to spray, and when to start his harvesting. This is decided by a company scientist with an instrument called a 'tenderometer' which measures whether the vegetables are sufficiently tender for the company's standards. If they are, and a bonus payment for those with an optimum reading is included in the farmer's remuneration, they are carried aft in special tractor-drawn trailers to a 'vining' station where the pods are stripped and the pea enters a 90-minute cycle of operations at the end of which it will be frozen and ready for sale at any time during the next 11 months before the harvesting season begins again.

# JULY 23ʀᴅ - 29ᴛʜ 1962

## IN THE NEWS

**Monday 23**    **"Mosley Rally."** Fifty-five people were arrested when demonstrators wrecked a Fascist meeting of Oswald Mosley's Union Movement in Trafalgar Square yesterday.

**Tuesday 24**    **"Telstar! Biggest Ever TV Triumph."** Millions of viewers in Britain shared in the first live programme to be beamed from America through Telstar, the Space satellite.

**Wednesday 25**    **"Britons in Race Up the Eiger."** Six men, at least two of them Brits, are making a desperate attempt to scale the Eiger mountain's "Murder Wall."

**Thursday 26**    **"Policy Outline Expected."** Mr Macmillan is to tell MPs in today's 'no confidence' debate that the Party must gain lost ground by unveiling its new progressive policies..

**Friday 27**    **"Three Die in Storm Havoc."** Lightning killed three people yesterday as fierce thunderstorms swept southern England. Holiday makers fled from the torrential downpours as they swept across much of the south coast.

**Saturday 28**    **"Stirling Moss Recuperates in the Bahamas."** Moss, seriously injured at Goodwood on Easter Monday, who then spent one month in a coma and remains partially paralysed, has gone to Nassau for four weeks convalescing in the sun.

**Sunday 29**    **"Deadlock in the Common Market Talks."** Crisis as both sides refuse to budge on the temperate agricultural exports from the Commonwealth.

## HERE IN BRITAIN

### "Strain of Caring for the Elderly."

A panel of helpers, paid and unpaid, who would act as "Relatives Anonymous" in caring for the aged or sick, is proposed in a report published this week.

These "friends of the family" would be required to help in households which needed them by taking over for a few hours at a time; by sharing the responsibility and, by sympathetic listening, providing a safety valve for the caring relative.

The report believes that there are many people who would be glad to do such work. Such a service would be valuable for those living alone and take the pressure off local authorities.

## AROUND THE WORLD

### "Fatal French Train Crash"

At least 38 people were killed and 52 injured today when five coaches of the Paris-Marseilles express were derailed near Dijon. One of them plunged over a 130ft. viaduct into the river valley.

Many of the casualties were believed to be Parisians going for holidays on the Riviera. Rescue workers with oxy-acetylene equipment had to cut through the twisted metal wreckage to free the trapped passengers.

The 16-coach train had left Paris at 12.30pm and had just emerged from a long tunnel and was travelling round a curved approach cutting to cross the viaduct when the derailment occurred.

# CLIMBER DIES ON EIGER

Barry Brewster, died on the Eiger mountain (13,026ft.) early Wednesday, whilst his climbing partner, Brian Nally was rescued by two other Britons, Chris Bonington and Don Whillans, who abandoned an attempt to be the first Britons to conquer the Eiger north wall to aid their fellow countryman. Nally came down the north face roped between them, amid thunder showers and rockslides, to the railway tunnel which runs through the Eiger.

Nally told journalists that Brewster had died in the early hours of the morning, before his body fell for a second time. "He was hit in a rock fall, and fell past me; it was terrible. Before he lost consciousness, he kept on saying, 'I am sorry Brian, I am sorry '." Brewster's first fall occurred last night when the two climbers were about half- way up the north face. He slithered and somersaulted about 200ft. on to the second icefield, where Nally was seen standing almost astride him to shield him from the rock falls that followed his slip. Nally then hacked out a bivouac for his injured comrade on the icefield.

Bonington and Whillans, who were already attempting to climb the north wall abandoned their own climb and reached Nally at about midday. The British rescuers had a half-day start over a Swiss team of nine men who left here at dawn. The Swiss, directed by a portable radio transmitter from the hotel, set up a rope line across the Interstoisser Traverse, one of the biggest obstacles on the lower slopes, to aid the three Britons but turned back after they saw Brewster fall and Nally start down on his own with Bonington and Whillans approaching.

## IN THE NEWS

**Monday 30**    "**Crowd Bowl Over Mosley.**" Sir Oswald Mosley's (Right wing) Union Movement march became a brawl where he was knocked to the ground, punched and had stones and fruit thrown at him.

**Tuesday 31**    "**Telstar Shines Again.**" BBC Panorama used the satellite for twenty-five minutes to bring viewers an edition from America.

**Wed 1st August**    "**Leonardo Saved for the Nation.**" The Government is contributing £350,000 towards the £800,000 the Royal Academy requires for the Leonardo da Vinci drawing which will otherwise be sold to a private collector.

**Thursday 2**    "**UK Bans Entry of Nazi Delegates.**" Permission to enter Britain is refused for those planning to attend the National Socialist World Conference planned for later this month.

**Friday 3**    "**American Spy to be Deported to US.**" The UK says no to giving the fugitive Dr Soblen, convicted in America of spying for Russia, asylum in Britain.

**Saturday 4**    "**The Queen Mother's Birthday.**" She spent her birthday in Yorkshire to present new colours to the 4th Battalion the King's Own Yorkshire Light Infantry.

**Sunday 5**    "**Scientist Dies at Secret Germ Centre.**" An inquiry is to be held following his death from 'pneumonic plague' – a form of The Black Death - at the Porton Microbiological Research Establishment near Salisbury.

### HERE IN BRITAIN

**"Pilot's Daring Sea Landing Saves Soldier "**

An air-sea rescue pilot based at Prestwick, Scotland, landed a seaplane in 7ft waves to take a sick soldier off a troopship 70 miles out at sea.

Landings are not normally attempted in waves more than 3ft and the pilot admitted, "This was my toughest assignment, I've only once before touched down in the open sea and that was the Mediterranean where conditions were calm.

The pilot had to use his emergency jet-assisted take-off, blasting half a mile across the sea before he could finally pull clear of the heaving waves.

### AROUND THE WORLD

**"A Welcome To Calypso Isle "**

Princess Margaret and Tony Armstrong-Jones were greeted by Jamaica's premier.

The Princess, in Jamaica for the island's independence celebrations, was given a tremendous welcome as she drove the twenty miles from the airport into Kingston. Yelling, cheering crowds broke through police cordons to run behind her open car.

Children threw flowers into her lap as she drove past, shouting "Welcome Princess, sister Missus Queen!" Police lining the route gave up hope of controlling the crowd and a surging mass of Jamaicans danced along behind the car.

# SOAP BOX WAR IN WEYMOUTH

*Trains At Weymouth Station 1962*

There is a war in Weymouth during the holiday season between taxi drivers and boys with hand carts and soap box carts. The soapbox boys aged between six and fifteen meet arriving holidaymakers at Weymouth station and offer their transport service to take the visitor's luggage to their hotel. On the last Sunday of July 1962 every coach of every train from the Midlands and the North was met by boys offering their 'much cheaper than a taxi' service. Some are earning £7 on a busy day.

The town's sixty taxi drivers are getting angry! They claim the boys are waylaying visitors before they can get to a taxi and that in their eagerness to get trade they are "hustling one another off vantage points, to the prejudice of good order generally and sometimes creating traffic risks". The taxi drivers are asking the town council to put an end to the "trade".

Said one, "*To put it mildly, the soapbox boys are a menace. Already, one of the soapboxes has been accidentally crushed under a taxi's wheels. The boys fight tooth and nail to get to holidaymakers before we do.*" They complained too, that visitors are pestered where-ever they are seen carrying baggage. Old ladies seem to be the best customers.

But the service doesn't always come up to expectations. One local resident told how he's seen a six year old boy walking beside his "taxi" while the holidaymaker client did the pushing!

It is not easy money. Each fare means an average walk of one mile. Often the journey is six miles both ways.

# Aug 6th - 12th 1962

## IN THE NEWS

**Monday 6** — "**Marilyn Monroe: Death Looks Like Suicide.**" The thirty six year old Hollywood star was found dead in bed late behind the locked doors in her luxury bungalow in the evening of Saturday, August 4, 1962, at her 12305 Fifth Helena Drive home in Los Angeles, California. She died of a barbiturate overdose .

**Tuesday 7** — "**Scotland Yard Hunt Barred Nazi.**" Special Branch joined the hunt for George Lincoln Rockwell, the American Nazi Party leader who slipped into Britain last week.

**Wednesday 8** — "**Historic Scene in Jamaica's Parliament.**" Following the Island's Independence from Britain on Monday, Princess Margaret presided at the state opening of their first Independent Parliament.

**Thursday 9** — "**Policeman Shot in Cinema.**" A detective was shot in the office of a West End cinema whilst hundreds, unaware of the drama, watched "South Pacific".

**Friday 10** — "**Second Wall Goes Up in Berlin.**" East Germans reinforce the Berlin Wall. Now it is 7ft thick in places, with barbed wire & broken glass on top and so high it blocks the view and with few exceptions, does not allow people to wave across it.

**Saturday 11** — "**The Duke Escapes by Inches.**" Watching his yacht being winched up at Cowes the Duke of Edinburgh jumped aside to save himself from being crushed by a falling crane.

**Sunday 12** — "**Boy Raiders Made Jemmies at School.**" A gang of Bournemouth school boy housebreakers stole more than £200 worth of property in five months.

## HERE IN BRITAIN

### "A Union Row Blows Up At The Palace"

Eighteen of the Queen's servants have complained to their Union claiming there is Army regimentation including parades and "too much spit and polish" in the Royal Mews where they work. Also their recently rearranged duties have hit many "spare-time" jobs as barmen, waiters and caretakers which they have taken to supplement their wages by between £8 and £11 a week.

The men, many of whom are known personally to the Queen, have between them more than 150 years of service to the Crown. They claim that the "spirit of loyalty and service to the Queen is being destroyed".

## AROUND THE WORLD

### "Thumbs Up And The Job Is Yours"

Selection by measurement of bodily proportions is being used for assessing applicants for jobs with a Paris electrical firm.

To qualify for a job, the length of a man's thumb should be the height of his ear. Arms, hands, legs and feet must all be in proportion, too.

The firm uses what throughout history has been called 'the golden mean', calculated by early mathematicians. Any significant disproportion is said to indicate some departure from the desirable norm in the character and emotional traits of the individual.

# SCREEN LEGEND DIES

Marilyn Monroe, the film actress, was found dead in bed in her Los Angeles home this week. The local coroner said the circumstances indicated a "possible suicide". Miss Monroe, aged 36, had long been suffering from nervous trouble arising from both her professional and her personal life.

The police said Miss Monroe was found by two doctors, who had to break a window to get into her room. She was lying nude in bed with the sheet pulled up to her neck and a telephone in her hand. On the bedside table were bottles of medicines, including an empty bottle of sleeping pills.

Marilyn Monroe began life as Norma Jean Baker in Los Angeles, where she was born on June 1, 1926. She was brought up in an orphanage and a series of foster homes, married first at the age of 15 and obtained a divorce four years later and began a career as a photographers' model. From this, in a few months, she graduated to a screen test with Twentieth-Century Fox, was given a contract- and the name which she was to make famous.

She said: "*Fame to me is only a temporary and a partial happiness-even for a waif, and I was brought up a waif. But fame is not really for a daily diet, that's not what fulfils you. It warms you a bit, but the warming is temporary.... "I was never used to being happy, so that wasn't something I ever took for granted. I did sort of think, you know, marriage did that.*"

Her three marriages, first to Los Angeles police officer James Dougherty, secondly to baseball star Joe di Maggio, and thirdly to the playwright Arthur Miller, all ended in divorce.

# AUG 13TH - 19TH 1962

## IN THE NEWS

**Monday 13**     "**Spacemen Meet 100 Miles Up**." Russia has two men in space making joint orbits. They have seen and spoken to each other whilst travelling at 1800mph.

**Tuesday 14**     "**Berlin Crowds Stone Russians**." On the first anniversary of the wall going up, over a thousand West Berliners marched flinging rocks into East Berlin and shouting "freedom."

**Wednesday 15**  "**Esso Petrol War with Shell and BP**". Esso will reduce the price of petrol at midnight, down a penny (0.5p) a gallon making regular, 4s 4d a gallon (5p a litre)

**Thursday 16**     "**PCs 'Drunk' in Secret Test**." In Reading, police were testing a secret apparatus called a "breathalyser", used to detect drunkenness. Motorists will be asked to blow into the machine which then indicates if they are 'over the limit'. If so, they have to go to the police station for a blood test.

**Friday 17**     "**Tornados Release 'Telstar'**". Billy Fury's backing band, The Tornados, release their instrumental record named after the communications satellite.

**Saturday 18**     "**Spy Planes for Britain**." The Air Ministry said, "The American reconnaissance plane the U-2's mission is solely to carry out high altitude weather research."

**Sunday 19**     "**Soviets Barred from the Air Show**." The Government is to ban Russia from the Farnborough Air Show in a "Tit for tat" row as we cannot look at their aircraft factories.

## HERE IN BRITAIN

### "The Mini's Big Brother"
The British Motor Corporation unveiled their Morris 1100, the long- awaited "big brother" to the Mini this week. Aimed at countering the Volkswagen's success in world markets, it is a ruggedly built machine that will cost under £700 in Britain.

It's shorter than the Morris 1000 – so easy to park and has almost as much passenger space as the Morris Oxford – so a comfortable four-seater. The revolutionary rubber and water suspension gives it limpet-like road holding.

It will cruise comfortably and quietly at 70mph and flat out, at nearly 80mph.

## AROUND THE WORLD

### "The Truth About The Striped Nudists"
Three men basking in the sun at a nudist colony just did not look right. They hadn't got the same tan as the naked holidaymakers sitting around them. The difference was a tell-tale pale strip around the trio's midriffs.

Then the bare truth came out. The three men were deserters from the French Foreign Legion who had taken cover – or rather uncover – with the nudists.

The deserters, all Germans, had posed as foreign tourists during their stay. They are among more than 200 Legionnaires who have deserted since their 2,000-strong regiment arrived in Corsica this summer.

# MONT BLANC IS BORED

Italian workers greeted a Frenchman after the last rock barrier separating the two teams constructing the Mont Blanc road tunnel had been blasted away. Workers from both sides, followed by local dignitaries, scrambled across the debris to fall into each other's arms in congratulation and excitement.

Helmets and garments were exchanged between workers who climbed across the boulders to embrace each other, enveloping themselves in their respective flags. Champagne was served by Chamonix casino waiters, retaining their dignity in miners' helmets, at a buffet in the heart of the mountain. Senior customs officials from both countries, there to record where the frontiers lay, looked on benignly. For the workers on the French side the celebrations were also for bonuses of up to £100 each.

The official opening ceremony will take place next month. Much work remains to be done, however, before the tunnel, begun in mid-1959, can be opened to traffic some time in 1964. Although the Italians were the first to reach the half-way mark, the last mile of their section is blasted only to just over half width. The concreting must be completed, the roads built, the immense ventilation systems installed, and the scale of tolls fixed.

When it is ready the tunnel will offer an all-the-year motor route from Paris to Rome, 130 miles shorter than is at present available. However, it will have only two traffic lanes-one in each direction, and two pedestrian pavements. With a speed limit of 30 miles an hour, no more than 400 vehicles an hour can be expected to pass through.

# AUG 20TH - 26TH 1962

## IN THE NEWS

**Monday 20** — "**Call for UN to Quit Berlin.**" Mr Krushchev has called for the withdrawal of troops belonging to Nato countries from West Berlin claiming they are provoking his forces.

**Tuesday 21** — "**Sir Winston Leaves Hospital.**" He left with a broad smile, a V sign and cigar in hand after 54 days recovering from the broken thigh he suffered on holiday in Monaco.

**Wednesday 22** — "**Another Baby for Princess Margaret.**" Princess Margaret had a baby girl 'Sarah' to be known as Lady Sarah Armstrong-Jones. Her first child, a son christened David Armstrong-Jones, also known as Viscount Linley, was born on November 3rd 1961

**Thursday 23** — "**Shots Fired at General De Gaulle.**" The French President escaped another attempt on his life when his car was hit by automatic fire near Paris.

**Friday 24** — "**Sharp Rise in Unemployment.**" 64,000 more people registering as unemployed since mid-July has made it the worst August since 1948 with now, 2.1% out of work.

**Saturday 25** — "**Shut Down Threat to London Docks**." On Monday the Tugmen and Lightermen who handle around half the cargo in London docks, start a strike unless they get more pay.

**Sunday 26** — "**Mystery Warships Shell Cuba.**" Two unidentified ships shelled Havana last night and Fidel Castro, Cuba's Premier accused the US of "a cowardly attack".

## HERE IN BRITAIN

### "Fewer Russian Tourists"

Encouraged by the record number of about 600 Russian visitors who last year came to Wales, five delegates from Wales visited Kiev, Leningrad, and Moscow. Each met the cost of about £80 to £90 from his own resources. One of them said, "The object was to promote more tourism between Wales and Russia". But according to the tourist board, not one party of Russian tourists has come to spend a holiday here since the visit.

Apparently, Wales is not alone. During the first six months of last year 1,707 visas were issued to Soviet tourists to visit England. In the second half of the year the number was 1,266. From January I to June 30 this year only 18 tourist visas were issued on request!

## AROUND THE WORLD

### "The George Cross Island Wants Freedom"

Malta's Premier this week demanded that the George Cross Island should be given its independence. His announcement follows Britain's rejection of his request for greater aid for the colony's economy which is facing a decline because of the reduction in employment in the island's Naval Dockyard. The Premier wanted £5m and was offered only £100,000.

"I did not come here to make a silver collection," he said, "the door has been slammed on Malta and the island would be in a stronger position to tackle it's problems as an independent member of the Commonwealth."

# BLITZ ON LICENCE DODGERS

The GPO has started its most intensive war yet against viewers who watch without buying their £4 licence. Nine new cars have "Television Detector" in large gold letters on both sides and at the back with an impressive 4ft revolving aerial.

A list of licence holders in each area goes with the detector car on its prowl. *"It's the homes that are not on that list that we check on,"* says the Post Office. One of the telly tecs said, *"These new cars have equipment far superior to any in the detector vans we've used so far. In open country we can pick up a set that is turned on two miles away. In a built-up area, we can pick them up at half a mile. At normal operating range – in the same street, or an adjoining one – we can not only tell on what side of the room the set is, but whether it is tuned to ITV or BBC".*

Some think the detector vans are designed merely to scare people into taking out licences and admittedly the Post Office advertise locally two weeks in advance that they are making a licence "comb". However, the tecs like to tell this story – "A detection squad was being watched by a crowd in a local street. *"Lot of nonsense,"* said one bystander, *"they can't find anything. I'm a radio engineer and I know."* Later that evening, he was of course "detected" at home!

Even better is the story of the bloke running out of his back garden, TV set in his arms after the detectors had knocked on his front door. In the back lane, he ran slap into a man, *"Better get yours, chum,"* he panted, *"the detector van's here."* "Chum" was a second TV detective!

## IN THE NEWS

**Monday 27** — **"Britain in Rumpus Over Raid on Cuba."** Britain became involved in the row over the shelling of Havana as the US said the boats sailed from the Bahamas – a British colony.

**Tuesday 28** — **"Now a Space Race to Venus."** Yesterday, America's robot Mariner was launched on its 181 million mile journey which aims to pass very close to Venus.

**Wednesday 29** — **"A Kick for Dr Beeching"**. He was greeted by catcalls and jeers from 300 railwaymen demonstrating against cuts, and then a man ran up and kicked him on the thigh.

**Thursday 30** — **"A New Nation in the Caribbean."** After nearly 150 years under British rule, Trinidad and Tobago becomes independent at midnight.

**Friday 31** — **"Two Britons Conquer the Eiger."** Chris Bonington and Ian Clough beat the mile-high treacherous North Wall of the 13,040ft Eiger. They became the first Britains to climb this classic route up the famous Alpine mountain.

**Sat 1st Sept** — **"Bomb at a Synagogue."** A bomb exploded in the forecourt of a Stoke Newington synagogue just forty minutes after the end of a service attended by a hundred worshippers.

**Sunday 2** — **"East End Fights at Fascist Meeting."** Police stopped the meeting in Bethnal Green two minutes after Sir Oswald Mosley began to speak and fighting broke out.

### HERE IN BRITAIN

#### "Naughty Northern Nudes"

Three nude paintings were back in their places in an Arts Council exhibition in Bradford, at the end of last week.

The paintings were banished to a locked room on Monday after 62-year-old Alderman Hird, master steeplejack and chairman of the Bradford Art Gallery Committee, had described them as "an affront to common decency. Children might see them."

His decision was reversed by his committee after a private viewing of the controversial paintings, which were taken by van to the town hall. After a sixty-five-minute meeting, the committee, which has three women members, voted by nine votes to five to have them returned to the exhibition.

### AROUND THE WORLD

#### "Dying Spy To Be Deported"

Dr Robert Soblen, the dying Russian spy, has lost his legal battle to stay in Britain. The Court of Appeal this week dismissed his challenge against a deportation order.

Soblen, sentenced to life imprisonment by an American court, got bail for an appeal and fled to Israel. While being flown back to America he was landed at London Airport suffering from self-inflicted wounds which meant he went to a London hospital.

But the last has not been heard of him, he is likely to be deported to America next week but the Home Secretary has offered to consider arguments on why the deportation order should not be enforced.

# MORE TEENAGERS MARRY

More teenagers than ever are getting married, the number has doubled in the past ten years, but there are fewer "shotgun" weddings than most people think.  In 1960 more than a quarter of British brides were teenagers. In a national marriage survey comparing 148 marriages of the 1950s in which the brides were under 20 years of age with 393 in the most popular marriage group, 20 to 24. The survey revealed that 31 per cent of the teenage brides and 13 per cent of the older ones were pregnant on marriage. The pregnant teenage brides showed few distinctive social or educational characteristics

Over half of the 46 pregnant teenage brides were under 19, the age at which three-quarters of the "prudent" chose to marry. Their pregnancy had led most of them to avoid white weddings, but it had not prevented them holding wedding receptions. More than half had been "going steady" with their future husbands for more than a year. Engagements of three months or less were the lot of only 14 of the 46 pregnant brides, suggesting that not more than about one-tenth had marriage forced on them by pregnancy alone.

Teenage couples were likely to have rather worse than average accommodation at  the start of marriage and more likely to become encumbered with children, which might help to explain why national figures showed that marriages with teenage brides ran about twice the risk of ending in divorce as those of brides in their early twenties. Even so over 80% of all teenage marriages would remain intact, compared with more than 90% of those with older brides. Also post-war marriages in general were rather less likely to end in divorce than those of the war or just pre-war years.

# SEPT 3ʀᴅ - 9ᴛʜ 1962

## IN THE NEWS

**Monday 3**  "**Persian Quake Kills Thousands**." Villages were wiped out and as many as 10,000 people killed in a devastating earthquake in central Persia at the weekend.

**Tuesday 4**  "**20,000 Germans Guard De Gaulle**." Police, a group of doctors and a food taster are on stand-by to protect De Gaulle from OAS killers when he arrives in Bonn for a State visit tomorrow.

**Wednesday 5**  "**Three Killed in Manx Grand Prix**." A black day as there were three deaths in yesterday's motorbike GP race on the Isle of Man's famous TT course.

**Thursday 6**  "**Jay Walkers to be Fined**." The transport minister has asked three London boroughs to make jay-walking an offence with fines as much as £50.

**Friday 7**  "**Russian Spy Dodges Deportation Again**." Robert Soblen was in a coma in Hillingdon Hospital having overdosed on sleeping pills as he was due to leave Britain for the USA.

**Saturday 8**  "**Kennedy Asks for Powers for Call Up**." The President asked Congress for authority to mobilise 150,000 reservists because of the "critical" situation in Berlin and Cuba.

**Sunday 9**  "**Gaitskell Says: No EU Yet**." The Labour leader made his Party's most clear-cut pronouncement on the European Common Market. On the basis of what has been agreed so far, it would cause great damage in the Commonwealth.

## HERE IN BRITAIN

### "The Artful Dodgers Are Dying Out"

The ancient art of Picking Pockets is dying out in Britain because youngsters are not prepared to spend sufficient time practising it,

The Police Review, said this week, "The veterans of the underworld deplore the fact that pocket-picking, card sharping and other dubious trades, do not attract the young criminals who are not prepared to wait until they are proficient at these crimes of skill .

If the decline continues, "we may well reach a situation in this country in which all the best pockets are picked by foreigners!"

## AROUND THE WORLD

### "Aid For Quake Victims"

Britain this week gave £10,000 to the Persian Government (Iran) to help earthquake relief work and The British Red Cross is to fly medical supplies worth £1,000 and a half ton of blankets to Tehran.

The US Air Force is rushing out 185 US Army doctors and nurses and more than 350 tons of supplies in "the biggest short-notice mercy mission in modern times."

Some of the planes are carrying blankets, tents and medicines as well as medical teams and badly needed water purification equipment.

# VINTAGE CAR AUCTION

*Rolls-Royce Silver Ghost*

A total of 119 privately owned veteran and vintage cars were auctioned for £49,000 in rural Scotland this week. The top price of £3,100 was paid for the six- cylinder 1910 Rolls-Royce shooting brake owned by the Duke of Windsor when he was Prince of Wales. The Canadian buyer has added it to a collection of 60 vehicles, including cars formerly owned by Mussolini, Charles Lindberg and Al Capone.

Prices at the auction were higher than had been expected and over 1,000 collectors came from many parts of the world. The old vehicles overflowed out of two large barns. Some people perched on top of cattle stalls and on bales of hay to watch the bidding but eventually many of them settled down in the seats of the old cars, giving the place the appearance of the starting point for the Brighton rally. The crowd mostly looked as if they might be stopping on their way to a point-to-point meeting. Checks were bold and there were deer- stalkers, duffel coats and shooting sticks, men with cravats at their throats and dogs at their heels.

However, the goods on sale were more diverse and piquant than their admirers. There were scout cars, dog carts, parcel vans and old beauties, brassy and sometimes over painted. Foremost among the buyers was an agent for William Harrah, owner of a large chain of casinos in Nevada. The Harrah collection numbers about 680 vehicles and the agent bought 11 cars for about £5,500. A Danish Baron bought several to add to his collection of 20, two of which were discovered walled up inside his own castle. A Rolls-Royce specially built for the late Eva Peron fetched £1,150. It has bullet- proof windows and armour plating in the rear compartment but not in the driver's position. Another Rolls Royce, once owned by Andrew Carnegie, the philanthropist was sold for £1,250.

# Sept 10<sup>th</sup>·16<sup>th</sup>1962

## IN THE NEWS

**Monday 10**    "**Hard Bargaining.**" Britain's entry into the Common Market will take up the first week of the Commonwealth Prime Ministers' Conference which opens today.

**Tuesday 11**    "**Spy Dies After Five Days in Coma.**" The American convicted spy, Robert Soblen died in Hillingdon Hospital last night before he could be extradited to the USA.

**Wednesday 12** "**A Million on the M1**". Another £1.5m is to be spent repairing extensive cracks on the concrete surfaced parts of the M1, less than 3 years since it opened. MPs called for an investigation into why these repairs were needed so soon. Was the initial construction sub-standard?

**Thursday 13**    "**Macmillan's Cabinet Call.**" To consider strategy following the Commonwealth Prime Ministers' adamant opposition to his Common Market plans.

**Friday 14**    "**Admiralty Man on Charge.**" A civil servant appeared in court yesterday on charges under the "Official Secrets Act," of recording secret information at the Admiralty.

**Saturday 15**    "**Rocket Fins Still Made**." A month after the cancellation of the Blue Water Rocket contracts, fins for the missile are still being made, drilled with holes and scrapped.

**Sunday 16**    "**Hover Trips Off.**" The world's first public Hovercraft service, opened in July between Rhyl and Wallasey, was closed yesterday with engine troubles. It was not due to close until tonight for scheduled engineering works.

## HERE IN BRITAIN

### "Storm Over Ban On Telephones"

New residents of Hemel Hempstead were told by the GPO that they cannot have private phones unless they promise not to use them between 9.30 – 11.30 am.

A spokesman said that the trouble was that the "new town" was growing too fast. "There has been a vast housing expansion in the area and the existing exchange will be exhausted before the new automatic one is ready."

What about an urgent call during the peak hours? "The caller will have to convince the operator it is urgent before it is put through!"

## AROUND THE WORLD

### "Roger Cycles To The Arctic"

Back home this week was a 16-year-old schoolboy from a cycling holiday. He travelled 4,500 miles, rode alone for six weeks and his trip took him to Norway's North Cape, 300 miles inside the Arctic Circle.

His dream of a journey to the land of the midnight sun began last summer when he read books about Norway, then he began saving his earnings from his paper round. He sailed to Bergen, then cycled 1450 miles north along the mountainous west coast to the North Cape. He returned on the gentler 1500 mile route through Finland.

# CHINA SHOOTS DOWN U2

An American built U2 spy plane on a "routine reconnaissance mission" for the Chinese Nationalists was shot down over Communist China this week and caused confusion in America who at first denied that any U2s had been turned over to any other allied government.

On Formosa, where Chiang Kai-shrek – leader of the Nationalists - has his island base, his statement said the plane was one of a pair that had been bought from the American aircraft firm, Lockheeds, in 1960. The statement issued by the Nationalists said the planes had been bought "to find out about conditions on the Communist-held mainland and had been in use since December 1960." Later, the US State Department "remembered" the export licence granted to Lockheeds.

What the Americans never imagined was that the Chinese Communists would have the means to bring down a U2 which has a normal flying altitude of 60-90,000 ft. and a spokesman said, "I assume they must have surface to air missiles." Comment from New York is the assumption that it is the Russians who have supplied China with the same type of rocket used to shoot down American Gary Powers over Russia in 1960, on what was admitted to be, a spying flight.

Chiang Kai-shek is reported to have grounded his second U2 and is "temporarily" suspending any spy flights over Chinese communist territories, but the US Government is alarmed at the possibility that the Red Chinese might use this incident as an excuse to start bombing the Chinese Nationalist offshore islands.

# IN THE NEWS

**Monday 17**    "**Graham Hill Wins at Monza.**" His victory in the Italian Grand Prix yesterday, virtually settles his place as the eventual winner of the World Championship.

**Tuesday 18**    "**Air Chief Admits De Gaulle Plot.**" A French Air Force officer who made arrangements for the General's plane flights, has confessed to leading the plot to assassinate him last month.

**Wednesday 19** "**Customers to Pay Price of Power.**" Electricity rates will rise again to pay for the biggest expansion of the national grid ever launched by Britain's electricity industry.

**Thursday 20**    "**Macmillan Has Go Ahead from Commonwealth Leaders.**" The way is now clear for Britain to go ahead with negotiations for joining Europe.

**Friday 21**    "**Rail Anger Explodes.**" The National Union of Railwaymen call a "one day strike" for October 3, in protest at Dr Beeching's proposed massive cuts in the rail network. The report has identified 2,363 stations (55% of the total) and 5,000 miles (30% of the total) of railway line for closure and the loss of 67,700 British Rail jobs.

**Saturday 22**    "**New Deal on Jobs.**" Government plan to guarantee a minimum of one month's paid notice for workers who have been with a firm 5 years – and one month's notice to strike.

**Sunday 23**    "**British Society Girl Kicked Out of Italy.**" Adultery is a punishable offence in Italy and the adulterous Sonia Clive, wife of a famous Italian lover was deported.

## HERE IN BRITAIN

### "New Sports Car Tops 107 MPH"

Details of a new MG sports car were issued yesterday. It is the MGB with a top speed of nearly 110 m.p.h. An enlarged engine of 1.798 c.c. gives it 94 bhp which is a considerable improvement on the power of its predecessor, the MGA 1600.

The top speed limited by permissible engine speed of 6,000 rpm is just over 107 mph. The car can accelerate from standstill to 60 mph in 11.8 seconds and to 80 mph in 35 seconds. An occasional seat at the back can take two small children. The price is just under £950.

## AROUND THE WORLD

### "The Case Of The Million Lost Cars"

It was revealed to police delegates attending the Interpol Congress in Madrid, that at least 1m stolen cars have vanished without trace in the past five years and the position is so serious that Interpol are to set up their own stolen-car bureau.

The report showed that highly organised syndicates are operating between Europe, the Middle East and South America. Stolen cars have their identities changed in underworld garages then, complete with forged documents, they are shipped or driven to other countries.

# TWO MONTHS UNDERGROUND

A self-inflicted trial of endurance and courage was successfully completed this week by Michel Sifre a 23-year-old French geologist. He was brought to the surface, weak but triumphant, after spending more than two months camping alone 400ft. down the Scarasson pothole in the Maritime Alps, north of Nice. He had enough food to last two months and lived in a tent. He had no watch and his only means of communication was a field telephone linking him with a mountain police station to which he gave progress reports and time estimates.

He was the voluntary guinea pig in a scientific experiment sponsored by the Centre for Aeronautical Research and the French Alpine Club. The aim was to provide new information on the psychological and physical effects of prolonged solitude in extreme cold, humidity, and gloom.

He lost count of time, falling increasingly behind the calendar until last weekend when he thought he still had 20 days to go until September 15. He also lost his sense of colour and reported that the ink with which he wrote his observations, which he knew to be blue, seemed to him to be apple green. At the beginning, the physical discomforts, freezing temperatures, extreme humidity, and rock falls, seem to have depressed him and towards the end, he suffered bouts of dizziness, occasionally losing consciousness. It became, he reported, increasingly difficult to find his equipment and to remember what he was supposed to be doing. Eating became troublesome and he wearied at the thought of washing and at times he began to lose interest in survival altogether. Yet each time, at the telephone call, he rallied his spirits and declared himself determined to hold out for 20 days longer than were necessary.

It took four hours today for the team of "rescuers" to carry, hoist and lift him up the narrow shaft to the surface. *"It's good to feel the sky"*, he said on emerging, even though he was wearing dark goggles and had a blanket thrown over his head when he complained of prickling pains in the eyes. M. Siffre said the last 30ft. of his ascent were the worst time, but he admitted that *"alone at the bottom I wept and even sobbed"*.

# IN THE NEWS

**Monday 24** "First Woman County Court Judge." Mrs Elizabeth Lane QC attains the highest judicial office held by any woman in England and Wales.

**Tuesday 25** "Miracle in Mid-Atlantic: 48 Are Saved." They owe their lives to an international armada of mercy ships and planes who snatched them from an Atlantic "hell" of gale-lashed giant waves.

**Wednesday 26** "Liston Out In 126 Seconds." Challenger Sonny Liston won the heavyweight championship of the world by beating Floyd Patterson with a sensational first round knockout.

**Thursday 27** "Costa Brava Storm Horror." Floods following massive cloudbursts roared through towns killing over three hundred with many more are still missing.

**Friday 28** "Five Days to Go and National Rail Strike Still On." Now the Government is expected to advise firms in London to give non-essential workers the day off.

**Saturday 29** "Big Increase in Marijuana Smoking." Teenagers and 'long haired hippy' students are among London addicts with 102 arrests in the first quarter of this year. Police are worried that this could escalate into the use of more serious drugs such as heroin.

**Sunday 30** "Car Control Urged in National Parks." Beauty is being submerged by motorists and with the prospect of 17m cars on our roads by 1970. The Lake District National Park calls for urgent planning to cater for the surging tide of motorists.

## HERE IN BRITAIN

### "Ranks Go Into Dry Cleaning"

The Rank organisation is to open Britain's first chain of coin in-the-slot dry cleaning shops. The shops' automatic machines – which will be operated by the customer – will dry clean six pairs of trousers or eleven dresses for 8s (40p). To have the same amount of clothing dry-cleaned by conventional methods would cost at least four times as much.

Ranks are to provide a luxury service at their shops with music playing constantly, tea on sale from machines and there will also be comfortable chairs and plenty of magazines.

## AROUND THE WORLD

### "Large Scale Food Adulteration In Italy"

Italian local authorities are reported to be energetically pursuing the campaign against adulterated foods, after the shock caused by news that unscrupulous producers were at work on an unexpectedly large scale.

Consumers are worried that a simple meal of bread and cheese with a glass of wine might include such substances as cow's blood, methylated spirits, banana skins, acetic acid and palm oil, as well as fish glue, if the extreme allegations about the concoctions produced by the adulterators are borne out by tests.

# MOT Car Tests To Start

MINISTRY OF TRANSPORT

## TEST CERTIFICATE

The motor vehicle, of which the Registration Mark is *NJ 2037*, having been examined under section 65 of the Road Traffic Act, 1960, it is hereby certified that at the date of the examination thereof the statutory requirements prescribed by Regulations made under the said section 65 were complied with in relation to the vehicle.

Vehicle Testing Station Number *4930/2*

Signature *St James*

Date of issue *1 July 19 Sixty Six*

For and on behalf of *Trinity Line*

Date of expiry *30 June 19*

Serial Number of immediately preceding Test Certificate _____
(To be entered when the above date of expiry is more than 12 months after the above date of issue)

The following further particulars of the vehicle should be entered:

Make *M.G.*

If a goods vehicle, unladen weight _____ cwt.

Approximate year of manufacture *1932*

If not a goods vehicle, horse power or cylinder capacity of engine in cubic centimetres *8 HP.*

ST. JAMES
ABBOTT&LEE GARAGE
MEMORIAL ROAD
HANHAM, BRISTOL
TEL. 673532

KEEP THIS CERTIFICATE SAFELY
SEE NOTES OVERLEAF

---

Mr. Marples, Minister of Transport, announced this week that he intends making the testing of five-year-old cars compulsory by early next year. Testing will then be extended to all but new cars. Without a test certificate, cars will be unable to get a Road Fund licence.

Although the number of cars on the road has been increasing at the rate of 500,000 a year for the past four years and reached six million in 1961, the vehicle-testing stations expect to be able to cope with this new influx of second-hand cars without any problems.

An official of the Motor Agents' Association said yesterday: *"It can be done, provided the age limit is brought down progressively and reasonable warning is given. If anything, the problem up to now has been that the motor trade has geared itself to the tests and then found that the equipment installed has not been used to capacity."*

A guarded welcome to the Minister's announcement was given by the motoring organisations, although both doubted the effect of compulsory testing on the road accident rate. *"We feel that properly conducted spot checks throughout the country is a better system",* a Royal Automobile Club official said.

The Society of Motor Manufacturers and Traders said the tests were designed to encourage routine and regular maintenance. All items covered which include the brakes, lights and steering-should be checked at least once a year. The one-year test will bring Britain into line with other countries which have insisted on compulsory annual tests for some years.

# OCT 1ST -7TH 1962

## IN THE NEWS

**Monday 1**  "**Britain Clears Up After the Gales.**" In the West Country, this week sees the start of repairs to property, roads cleared of fallen trees and electricity to be restored after the weekend storms.

**Tuesday 2**  "**Minister of Transport TV Sensation.**" On television last night, Mr Marples intervened in the rail dispute and offered a meeting between the Railmen and Dr Beeching in a bid to avert tomorrow's strike.

**Wednesday 3**  "**Walk to Work**". Last minute talks between the rail unions and Dr Beeching failed and the train strike started at midnight.

**Thursday 4**  "**Labour Says 'No' to Common Market Terms**." Mr Gaitskell, persuaded the majority of delegates at the Labour Party Conference to back his opposition to Britain's entry.

**Friday 5**  "**Britain Rejects US Call for Shipping Boycott of Cuba.**" The Government says this partial blockade, in peace time, would not be justifiable in international law.

**Saturday 6**  "**Ice Cream Giants Start New Cold War.**" Three of the biggest and best-known names in the ice cream business in Britain are to merge into a giant Neapolitan sandwich. They are Lyons Maid, Neilson's and Eldoradolarge who are are merging to fight Unilever's giant "Stop Me and Buy One" Wall's brand.

**Sunday 7**  "**Hospitals in Cash Crisis.**" Owing to rising costs, Britain's hospitals have run through their cash allocations this year faster than ever before.

## HERE IN BRITAIN

### "3,000 Bombs Cleared By Navy Team"

Bombs, mines, shells, torpedoes and other explosive objects from the last War, are still being cleared from the coasts of Britain at the rate of more than 3,000 a year by the Royal Navy's bomb and mine disposal team from H.M.S. Vernon.

The team are ready at any time but it is during the summer months that they are at their busiest. Holidaymakers on the beaches find bombs, report them to the police, and the bomb disposal men at Portsmouth are called. In the past fortnight the team have travelled thousands of miles to clear explosives between the Wash and the Devon coast.

## AROUND THE WORLD

### "The Pope's Pilgrimage By Train"

Thousands of people this week cheered the Pope as he carried out his pilgrimage by train to the Marian sanctuary at Loreto and on to Assisi.

He became the first reigning Pope to use the Vatican railway station, taking the presidential train placed at his disposal by President Segni. He was accompanied by 25 dignitaries of his court, including four Cardinals.

The purpose of his journey is to invoke the help of the Madonna and St. Francis for the successful outcome of his Ecumenical Council which opens here next Thursday.

On Monday, the US Government established order after more than 12 hours skirmishing with racialist rioters at the University of Mississippi, during which at least two people lost their lives and about 75 were injured. Federal marshals, troops, and military policemen cleared the university campus by 4.30 that morning and went then to the centre of the town where, after a brief gun battle, they cordoned off the main square and set up roadblocks.

At the university administration building, where a nine-hour battle was fought with tear gas, stones, bottles, and fire hoses, nearly 200 prisoners were brought in with their hands up. By mid-morning the town of Oxford was empty, shops were closed, few people were on the streets and the square was patrolled by troops with fixed bayonets.

Rioting had begun after it became known that federal marshals had brought a Negro applicant, James Meredith, on to the campus. Rioting continued overnight and early morning, with waves of tear gas being thrown by federal forces against stone-throwing demonstrators, who wrecked and burned dozens of cars. Troops pursued the gangs of demonstrators to the centre of the town, but this was the end of resistance, and the federal forces had a grip on the situation.

Later that morning, James Meredith was officially enrolled in the administration building. Outside the building, tear gas shells, glass, bricks, paper and burnt-out cars littered the ground while soldiers slept under trees and helicopters circled overhead.

Meredith walked to his first class amid angry, racist shouts but the slight 29-year-old student of political science made only one comment, *"This is not a happy occasion."*

# IN THE NEWS

**Monday 8**  "**Steel Industry Shut Down**". Michael Foot, MP for Ebbw Vale last night appealed to the TUC to settle the "who does what" dispute now threatening thousands of jobs. It is between bricklayers and steel workers as to who installs a new type of lining in furnaces.

**Tuesday 9**  "**Gem Raid: Big Five Hunt.**" Scotland Yard are hunting a gang who stole £100,000 worth of jewels in London's West End. They suspect five recently freed top cracksmen.

**Wednesday 10** "**Brickies Agree to Inquiry.**" The steel strike is averted but the Railmen say, 'our next strike will be longer'. At least a week is suggested and 'the sooner the better.'

**Thursday 11**  "**Britain's £96m Surplus.**" This has been the best half-year since 1959 with the value of goods exported moving strongly upwards since the beginning of the year.

**Friday 12**  "**Bridge Across the Panama Canal Opens Today.**" Since they were separated by the canal in 1914, North and South America are now linked by land again.

**Saturday 13**  "**London's Holy Lady Killed.**" Mary O'Donnell was found murdered in her 'Little Italy 'shop where she sold plaster Madonnas, prayer books, Bibles and crosses.

**Sunday 14**  "**Common Market Will Bring Changes but We Must Welcome Them.**" Prime Minister Macmillan received a standing ovation on the last day of the Conservative Party Conference in Llandudno.

## HERE IN BRITAIN

### "Grandma's Cat Could Be A Killer."

Britain's old people were warned yesterday by a senior physician at the Royal Institution of Public health, "Get rid of your cat, it could kill you!"

He said, "Cats seem to derive a highly sensuous pleasure by winding themselves round the legs of people, particularly in the dark or under a long dress. They are a constant menace to the stability of old women."

He said, "My choice for an old person's pet, is a budgie," and finished on a warning note, "old people also trip over their grandchildren but nothing can be done about them!" Dogs were thought to be a slightly less risky pet.

## AROUND THE WORLD

### "The Siege Of Monte Carlo"

The French threatened to "blockade" the Principality of Monaco when talks broke down over President De Gaulle's 'war on foreign tax dodgers' and the number of firms setting up in Monte Carlo where there is no income tax, so having an unfair advantage over the French.

Just after mid-night on Friday, French customs men arrived at the Monaco frontier where a huge crowd was waiting in pouring rain on both sides of the border.

A few cars were stopped but no-one was taking it too seriously, locals and the French swapped jokes and chatted. After forty minutes, the French went home!

Miss Margaret Hunter aged 65, a schoolteacher in Cheshire was on her 41st driving lesson but it was the first with Mr Davenport and she was quite upset when he stopped the car after only 15 minutes saying, "*This is plain suicide. I've had enough.*" Then off he walked leaving her alone in her new red Fiat at the side of the A6 at Stockport.

The learner driver said that night, "*I just don't understand it, I thought I was driving well. The car stopped and started a few times, but I thought that was a fault in the petrol system. All the other driving instructors have been quite helpful, I don't think Mr Davenport is the right man to teach people to drive, he seems so nervous!*" Two days later, driving with an experienced woman driver, she was in a collision with a four-ton lorry on the same road, the A6.

Finally on Saturday, her own car being too damaged, she took her driving test in a car belonging to "The Sunday People" newspaper - and she failed. The instructor told her, "*Don't be discouraged, many people fail on their first attempt. You must have more tuition*". Miss Hunter failed on reversing, turning, signalling, gear changing, braking, use of mirror and adjustments of speed to the road conditions. On her thirty-minute test she took ten minutes to start the engine, stalled the engine five times and reversed on the pavement whilst making a three-point turn.

Before the test she had said, "*I'm pretty confident of passing. I've been unlucky in the past that's all.*" After the test she said, "*Perhaps my nerves got the better of me, but the instructor was very nice, rather like a primary school teacher. I shall try again next month.*"

# OCT 15TH - 21TH 1962

## IN THE NEWS

**Monday 15** — "**Brussels Clashes.**" Flemings marched on Brussels campaigning for greater political and cultural rights for the Flemish and wider use of their language instead of French.

**Tuesday 16** — "**Bank Robber Vanishes.**" Just four hours after being sentenced to five years for stealing £1,000 and after only ten minutes in his cell in Leeds, the thief 'vanished'. Despite a widespread police search he remains at large, but is not believed to be dangerous.

**Wednesday 17** — "**Singing Crowds Demonstrate at Mandela's Trial.**" In Pretoria, the anti-apartheid activist is on trial for treason and bombings of government buildings.

**Thursday 18** — "**Strike Stops Fords.**" Just five days after the workers were given a 10s (50p) a week rise, the giant Ford motor factory at Dagenham was brought to a standstill when the night shift walked out.

**Friday 19** — "**Horror in Fog – Mass Crash on A38.**" Eleven people from two families died when their youth club mini-bus crashed into a lorry in Gloucestershire in thick fog. This was Britain's worst ever road traffic accident.

**Saturday 20** — "**Make Hospitals More Comfortable**" Enoch Powell, Minister of Health, says hospitals should replace the long, hard benches patients have to wait on with chairs.

**Sunday 21** — "**I**ndian and Chinese Troops Clash" Fierce fighting was raging along two disputed border areas in the Himalayas and in Kashmir .

## HERE IN BRITAIN

**"Sleep? – A Waste Of Telly Time."**

A Darlington school teacher wrote this week to parents telling them of his concerns at their listlessness. He believed this is due to their not getting enough sleep as the children regard sleep as a waste of good television time.

Two school doctors checked on the sleeping habits of 947 children and those staying up late did far worse in lessons than the average.

They suggested these bedtimes:
Under 7, in bed by 6.30pm. 7 to 8 by 7.00pm. 9 years by 7.15. 10 years by 7.30pm and 11 years by 7.45pm.

## AROUND THE WORLD

**"From Pigeon Post To Telstar Reuters Celebrations."**

As a prelude to Saturday's celebrations at the exact house in Aachen, where Baron Reuter launched, in 1850, the pigeon post service which laid the foundations of the famous British news agency, a conversation was held via Telstar between Aachen and New York.

The News Manager of Reuters exchanged greetings with the Managing Editor of the New York Times who said he thought this direct link between the US, the UK and Germany was the beginning of a new era of understanding.

# Humans To Live On Seabed

A forecast that a "new man" would be developed, probably over the next 50 years, was made by Jacques Cousteau at the second World Congress of Underwater Activities this week. He said that such a man – Cousteau spoke of him as "Homo Aquaticus" - would be able to exist without the use of his lungs, which would be filled with an inherent compressible liquid, and he would be able to withstand pressures at depths of 3,000 ft. to 5,000 ft.

Eventually hospitals would be established at the bottom of the sea and babies would undergo surgery at birth which would enable them to live thereafter under water as well as on land. *"There will be new parliaments and probably new nations living under water,"* Cousteau said, *"We have good reason to believe that sea mammals are animals that have returned to the sea."*

He spoke of a village *"which would be erected at varying depths in the sea next February or March. As many as two dozen people would live there, probably including himself. It would be erected with small nuclear plants to provide energy to draw respiratory gases from the sea and would have no physical connection with a land base".*

This opens up the possibility of under-sea housing whereby the diver could stay on the seabed for days, weeks, or months, gaining a large amount of time for the hours of decompression which must be spent afterwards. As the gases in the house would be at the pressure of the outside water, the divers could freely leave their house to go about their business and return after a working shift to the comforts of home.

# Oct 22ND - 28TH 1962

## IN THE NEWS

**Monday 22** — **"Smallpox Quarantine on British Liner."** Twelve hundred passengers were "imprisoned" aboard a British luxury liner off Naples because of a suspected case of smallpox.

**Tuesday 23** — **"US Fleet Cuts off Cuba."** America has begun blockading Cuba to stop Soviet arms reaching the island which is only 90 miles from Florida.

**Wednesday 24** — **"2,000 in Clash at Embassy."** Police were rushed to the American Embassy in London to battle with 'ban-the-bomb' demonstrators chanting, "Hands off Cuba."

**Thursday 25** — **"Soviet Ships Turn Back."** Some of the Soviet ships steaming towards Cuba have altered course after a message from Mr Khrushchev which said a 'summit' meeting with the USA would be helpful to defuse the crisis.

**Friday 26** — **"Shock Over Babies Born at Home."** At least 50 babies a week in Britain die unnecessarily because they are born at home without proper medical care.

**Saturday 27** — **"Emergency in India."** As Chinese troops crossed over the North-East border into the Himalayan region of Kashmir, Indian women are urged by the government to give up their gold so that the state can buy weapons.

**Sunday 28** — **"Spy Catchers name 'Sex Risk' Men."** A secret list prepared by detectives, name homosexual men who hold top Government posts as potential threats to security.

## HERE IN BRITAIN

### "Outing From A Jail – To Marry."

Dennis Stafford, the master escaper, was out of jail for a short spell this week to marry the girl he fell in love with five years ago when he was 'on the run' and who is the mother of his daughter.

He had escaped from Wormwood Scrubs prison, where he was serving a seven-year sentence for house breaking, and set up a textile business in Newcastle upon Tyne but, with the police on his heels, he fled to the West Indies.

Brought back to jail, he then escaped again, from Dartmoor, but was recaptured and since when his now, wife, had been visiting him.

## AROUND THE WORLD

### "Silly Protest On Ship Painting".

A long-standing dispute over the painting of ships by their crews when vessels are in port has raised its head again, this time in the Port of London.

A Swedish shipping company has received a warning from the Amalgamated Society of Painters and Decorators that they may call for a strike of dock workers if their ships' crews are seen painting their vessels in the port.

From their head office in Sweden the company replied "We have received your letter of the 24th inst., the contents of which we find extremely silly".

# FROM RUSSIA TO JAIL

**Moscow Kremiln, Red Square and St Basil Cathedral**

This week another spy went down from the dock in the Central Criminal Court to long years in prison the sombre words of the Attorney General, *"You have been well rewarded by those that have used you as their tool and you have sold some part of the safety and security of the people of this country for cash"*.

William Vassall, a £14-a-week Admiralty clerk was sentenced to a total of 18 years' imprisonment for offences under the Official Secrets Act. The Lord Chief Justice told him, *"I take the view that one of the compelling reasons for what you did was pure selfish greed. You have said in your statement to the police that you had no intention of harming this country."*

The Chief Justice continued , *"I am quite unable to accept that. A man of your education, intelligence and experience knew full well that this information and these documents would be directly of assistance to an enemy. I accept that at the inception of this you were subjected to threats of various kinds, but one cannot shut one's eyes to two matters. First, that when you came back to this country, when you could have made a clean breast of the matter, you did not do so. You chose to serve in a place where you could obtain information and pass it over."*

A committee of inquiry are now to find what went wrong and some of the questions they will ask are obvious. It is now apparent that Vassall was a security risk on three main counts. He had served behind the Iron Curtain as a bachelor, he is a homosexual and he lived, quite obviously, beyond his salary. While those responsible could hardly be expected to know all the details of his private life, it is not too much to expect that some suspicion should have been aroused.

## IN THE NEWS

**Monday 29** — "**Back From the Brink.**" The world came back from the brink of a nuclear war last night after Mr Khrushchev spoke to Mr Kennedy to ease the tension over the Cuba missiles.

**Tuesday 30** — "**India Accepts UK Military Assistance.**" First assignment of British arms arrives by air to help India resist and repel the Chinese in their border clashes.

**Wednesday 31** — "**Mr Wilson to Seek Deputy Labour Leadership.**" Harold Wilson last night stated his intention to challenge George Brown to become the Deputy Labour Leader.

**Thurs 1st Nov** — "**Dangers That Face the Church of England.**" Increasing bureaucracy and a public image of the church as a 'highly efficient big business concern'.

**Friday 2** — "**625 Line Colour in BBC Tests**". Full colour is to take over from black and white for the first time on some BBC television programmes next week.

**Saturday 3** — "**A Threat to Christmas Turkeys**". An outbreak of fowl pest in Lancashire has caused more than a million birds to be destroyed in the past two months.

**Sunday 4** — "**Six Snatched from Death in Wrecked Trawler.**" Six Frenchmen were rescued off Lands End after being trapped for over seven hours in the wreck of a Dieppe trawler.

## HERE IN BRITAIN

**"Paratroops Fall In Front Of Express Train."**

British parachute troops caught this week by gusting winds in a Norfolk night exercise began drifting down helplessly across the main Norwich to Cambridge railway line as a diesel express train approached. 170 British paras were dropped in pitch darkness from between l,000ft and 800ft.

Parachutes and harnesses were entangled in the telephone wires beside the track, bringing them down across the double line. Medical orderlies described how they dragged men clear only just in time from the path of the express.

One man who injured his ankle claimed that his boots scraped across the top of the train's carriages as he fell.

## AROUND THE WORLD

**"Reaching For Mars."**

Russia launched a spacecraft this week on a seven-month journey towards Mars, the planet most likely to support life.

Cameras will photograph the surface and relay pictures back to earth where scientists are hoping to settle the historic mystery of whether there is 'life on Mars'.

The planet has a diameter of 4,220 miles, is between 35-65 million miles away and has a year that lasts 687 earth days.

With luck, the spacecraft named Mars 1 will pass within a few thousand miles of the planet, close enough for the cameras and instruments to make their observations.

# NUCLEAR WAR AVOIDED

*A US Plane Monitors A Soviet Ship Carrying Missiles (centre of deck) To Cuba*

President Kennedy took a big gamble with world peace this month taking a tough line over the Russian bases in Cuba. Mr Khrushchev climbed down after an exchange of personal letters. President Kennedy told the Russian premier that now, "as we step back from danger," East and West could make real progress together in disarmament.

The world had been on the brink of nuclear war, and during this crisis, Mr Khrushchev raised the problem of bases in general. In his letter he states, *"Our aim has been, and still is, to help Cuba and enable the people to live in peace. You want to make your country safe. This is understandable, but Cuba too wants the same thing. All countries want to make themselves safe. But how are we, the Soviet Union, to assess your actions when you have surrounded with military bases the Soviet Union; surrounded with military bases our allies; have disposed military bases literally round our country; have stationed your rocket armament there? Your rockets are situated in Britain, situated in Italy, and are aimed against us. Your rockets are situated in Turkey. You are worried by Cuba. You say that it worries you because it is a distance of 90 miles by sea from the coast of America. But Turkey is right next to us. Our sentries walk up and down and look at each other. Do you consider, then, that you have the right to demand security for your own country and the removal of those weapons which you call offensive and do not acknowledge the same right for us?"*

Now, Mr Kruschev has ordered the dismantling of his Cuban bases under the supervision of the United Nations, accepting for the first time, the principle of on-site inspections carried out by the UN.

## IN THE NEWS

**Monday 5** — "**Maria's Golden Hour.**" The world's most famous opera singer, Maria Callas, thrilled millions of viewers last night in ATVs £25,000 triumph, 'The Golden Hour.'

**Tuesday 6** — "**Cheaper Cars Today – Big Tax Cut.**" The Chancellor, Reginald Maudling, slashed the purchase tax on new cars last night from 45% to 25%.

**Wednesday 7** — "**Hold That Strike.**" Talks are started to avoid a final showdown between 22 unions and the Ford Motor Co. and avert the official strike due to start in ten days' time. Expected increased demand for the cars, following yesterday's tax cut, has put added pressure on Ford to settle the dispute quickly.

**Thursday 8** — "**£10,000 Raid at Z Cars Studio.**" While actors in police uniform were rehearsing at the BBC television centre, real bandits attacked cashiers in the centre's pay office.

**Friday 9** — "**It's Victory for Brown by 30 Votes.**" George Brown keeps his job as Deputy Leader of the Labour party beating his challenger Harold Wilson in last night's ballot.

**Saturday 10** — "**Ford Wives on 'No Strike' Parade.**" Workers' wives, many pushing babies in prams, marched outside the plant at Dagenham in protest at next week's big strike. 'We'll be the ones to suffer,' they chanted."

**Sunday 11** — "**Mother Found Not Guilty.**" A young mother accused of killing her seven day old baby, severely deformed by the drug thalidomide, was acquitted in a Belgian court.

### HERE IN BRITAIN

**"Tommy Goes To The Palace Party."**

Tommy Steele, one of the kings of showbiz, and his wife Ann, a former dancer whom he married two years ago, were guests of the Queen and the Duke of Edinburgh at Buckingham Palace this week.

Quite a night to remember for the boy from Bermondsey who started off as a seaman before becoming a rock 'n' roller in Soho coffee bars.

He mingled with sixty other famous guests including Stirling Moss and his rally-driver sister Pat and Francis Chichester the Atlantic yacht adventurer.

### AROUND THE WORLD

**"Zsa Zsa Marries Husband Number Four"**

Wearing a pink, Balenciaga dress, the actress became the wife of engineering chief Herbert Hunter in New York. Her previous husbands were the Turkish diplomat Burham Belge Jye, the hotelier Conrad Hilton and actor George Sanders.

She said about her Mink coat, "It is not my best, but the only one that matches my dress."

She said about her new husband, "I first saw him dancing with another woman and decided to take him away from her."

Zsa Zsa is 37, and her new husband is 54.

# BRITISH CLOTHES TAKE OFF

*A Mary Quant Show At London Fashion Week*

The Changing of the Guard, Roast Beef of Old England, twin sets and tweeds was all fashion buyers thought about when passing through London on their way to Paris, Rome and Florence a few years ago. London was unknown as a big fashion centre. The London Fashion House Group consisting of 26 different fashion houses, made a bid to change all this by starting the London Fashion Week.

At first the buyers came and went – without buying. Four years later the courageous foresight and tenacity of the founders have paid off. When the eighth Show opened this week, buyers from 52 different countries, including China, were present. In one hour, 24 models showed off 250 'off the peg' garments expected to bring in around £900,000 of orders.

Europe is still Britain's largest customer for ready-to-wear clothes and so popular is the London merchandise at the moment, that a team of buyers from the Galleries Lafayette in Paris came over recently in advance of the openings, and placed orders with two members of the Fashion House Group, Polly Peck and Sambo, for 400 garments each. A useful beginning to the season.

Now, the Fashion House Group, in its bid to span the globe, opens a British Week in San Francisco next week, followed by a Week in Los Angeles. This is not, as maybe thought, a long way from the clothes for British women in shops and stores, as the livelier the export market, the better the general quality of the home trade in every way because it will allow improvements in manufacture, experiment and wider ranges of styles and fabrics.

# Nov 12ᵀᴴ - 18ᵀᴴ 1962

## IN THE NEWS

**Monday 12** — "**Russia Warns Britain.**" Moscow radio said, 'A new series of underground nuclear tests by Britain would complicate the achievement of the treaty to ban nuclear tests'.

**Tuesday 13** — "**Britain to Go Ahead with Nuclear Test in Nevada.**" The UK tells Russia the test is for essential military purposes and in no sense the start of "a new nuclear series".

**Wednesday 14** — "**Judge to Head Tribunal.**" After so many allegations and rumours arising from the Vassall Admiralty spy case, the Prime Minister has ordered an independent enquiry.

**Thursday 15** — "**The Big Ford Strike is Off.**" Talks to begin with management over the seventy workers blacklisted as 'troublemakers' by the firm.

**Friday 16** — "**MP to Press for Easier Divorce**". Leo Abse, Labour MP for Pontypool, private member's proposal is that courts should have the power to grant divorces in cases where couples have been living apart for seven or more years.

**Saturday 17** — "**40 Hour Week for Scottish Builders.**" A reduction of two hours per week with no loss of wages has been conceded by the employers.

**Sunday 18** — "**Stop the Big Drift South for Jobs.**" Labour party leader Hugh Gaitskell called for urgent Government action to stop the exodus of job-hungry northerners moving down south. He demanded more tax payer funded support for shipbuilding, mining and steel making.

---

## HERE IN BRITAIN

### "BBC 2 To Start In 1964"

It is hoped that the second channel of BBC television, branded as BBC2, will start in London in April 1964, and reach the north of England by the summer of 1965. BBC2 will begin with at least 25 hours 'fresh' material a week.

As part of their plan to give people "more of what they wanted at the hours when they could best see it", they envisaged longer plays, more domestic ballet, opera and science.

However there came a warning, "Colour", said the Director, "would always be very expensive and it was likely that there would never be more than an average of one or two hours a night" with the rest of the programmes in black and white.

---

## AROUND THE WORLD

### "Filming Drunken Drivers"

Police in Colorado are experimenting with taking films of motorists charged with drunken driving as soon as the driver arrives at the police station.

They say it is often difficult to paint in words, when giving evidence, a graphic picture of just how the defendant looked, spoke and behaved in the police station and a film taken at the time would give the court an exact record of what happened.

In Colorado, the percentage of drivers pleading guilty had risen in one year from 20 to 85. "They have seen the film the next morning and their plea has been influenced in consequence."

# SHOPS TO GO METRIC

The yard and the pound weight will henceforth be defined in terms of the metre and the kilogram. This was one of the President of the Board of Trade's statements this week in the Commons on the introduction of the Weights and Measures Bill, and it meant that in due course the hallowed copper yard and the revered platinum pound will be deposed from their position of primacy.

Worse news was to follow. The metre had recently been defined in terms of the wavelength of the light of krypton-86 which, as everyone will know, is an isotope of an inert gas discovered by Ramsay! A Labour MP was concerned, "*At the moment,*" he pointed out, "*local authorities had access to copies of the standards of measurement which were deposited at various places about the country. Could they say as much for krypton-86?* "

The new definitions, he said, would mean that the yard would be a fraction longer and the pound a fraction lighter - which, it might be remarked, is bad for the draper and good for the greengrocer. Schoolboys, but only young schoolboys, will no doubt be overjoyed to hear that those unmemorable units, the rod, pole, and perch, are to be banished in five years' time. The provisions of the Bill that relate to the sale of food and drink will guarantee customers a fairer deal than they are having at the moment.

The weight of the contents will in future be stamped on the outside of all packed goods which will help the housewife when trying to distinguish between the relative merits of jumbo, family, or economy sized packets and Englishmen will in future have a firmer guide to how large a large Scotch ought to be, though the Scots themselves will in all probability have larger ones still!

# Nov 19ᵀᴴ - 25ᵀᴴ 1962

## IN THE NEWS

**Monday 19**    "**Nine Die in Lifeboat Within Yards of Safety.**" A freak wave hit the Seaham, Co. Durham, lifeboat at the entrance to the port capsizing it and drowning nine crew members.

**Tuesday 20**    "**Air Lift of British Women and Children Starts.**" As the Chinese advanced into North-East India having surged across the Himalayas a month ago, Britain started to evacuate many of its citizens.

**Wednesday 21**    "**Cease Fire Sensation – China Calls Troops Back.**" Red China staggered the world by announcing her troops would stop fighting in India tonight. No reason was given.

**Thursday 22**    "**Cuba Blockade Ships Return to US.**" The blockade of Cuba by US ships came to an end when most of the task force returned to Atlantic ports.

**Friday 23**    "**Worst Unemployment Figures since 1959**". The total number of people registered as jobless was 544,451, nearly 2.5% of the total working population.

**Saturday 24**    "**Macmillan in Trouble After Election Shocks.**" The future of Mr Macmillan as Prime Minister is now in doubt following the disastrous by-election results this week when Labour won previously Conservative seats in Glasgow and South Dorset

**Sunday 25**    "**Found! After 24 hours alone on Dartmoor.**" A seven-year-old boy lost on Dartmoor was found cold and hungry and explained, "I was only chasing the ponies!"

## HERE IN BRITAIN

**"Forged Bank Notes – Printed In Broadmoor "**

Three people are on trial for passing £187 worth of imitation £1 and £5 notes which had been printed by the inmates of Broadmoor institution for the criminally insane, and passed on to visitors.

The notes were printed with official permission as "a kind of occupational therapy" for use by the prison concert party. "The prisoners have a very strong amateur dramatic group", the prosecutor said, "with two annual stage presentations and several musical productions involving up to 30 inmates".

As they are criminally insane the forgers are likely to escape further punishment.

## AROUND THE WORLD

**"Radio Carbon Dating Discoveries"**

It was announced at a radio carbon dating symposium that artificial satellites and rockets have made it possible for scientists to establish that 1,000 tons of extra-terrestrial dust reach the earth's surface every day.

It was also reported that by dating the hair of frozen mammoths found in the Arctic, it had been found that these animals had died 12,000 years ago.

Also established was that the waters of the Black Sea had turned from fresh to saline about 8,000 years ago when it became joined to the Mediterranean Sea.

# MOTHER HID SON IN ATTIC

The fantastic secret of widow Yvonne Vasseur was revealed this week. She had been hiding her son at home from the police for seventeen years. Her son Jacques, a former Nazi Gestapo chief, escaped after being condemned to death for war crimes in 1945. Jacques was twenty when the war broke out and he joined the Nazis, becoming chief of the Gestapo's French auxiliary force with the job of uncovering French resistance fighters.

At his trial in 1945 he was held responsible for the deaths of forty-four Resistance fighters massacred by German troops. Now he is in jail near his mother's home in Lille, France. Yvonne wept, telling friends, *"A mother will do anything for her son, I only did what I thought was best."*

During those seventeen years not even her neighbours had suspected anything even though they noticed Yvonne was never prepared to stop and gossip in the street. They never guessed the reason why the steaks she bought always seemed big for just one widow, or that she was washing a man's clothes secretly or cutting his hair. For more than 6,000 days Jacques had been sitting behind drawn curtains studying, listening to the radio and in recent years, watching television.

That was until this week when police called at the house to discuss a routine matter and he was not quick enough off the mark when they knocked and pushed the door which had been left open by mistake. Over his mother's shoulder, the police spotted a pale, thin, gaunt faced man in grey slacks and slippers. He spoke up, *"I'm the person you want."* Jacques told the police, *"Being shut up for 17 years like that was worse than prison. I learned nine languages to stop myself going mad."*

# Nov 26th - Dec 2nd 1962

## IN THE NEWS

**Monday 26**    "**Public Delighted with New BBC Satire.**" Anxious BBC officials were relieved to learn we all loved the new Saturday night revue, "That Was The Week That Was."

**Tuesday 27**    "**Ford Hesitates on Expansion Plans.**" The £8.5m extension to the nearly completed Liverpool plant is under threat because 'go slows', official strikes and demarcation disputes have hampered the work so far. Together with strikes and disputes at the Ford Dagenham factory, over a month's production has been lost so far this year.

**Wednesday 28**    "**Bowler Hatted Bandits.**" A gang of city types in bowlers, dark suits and neat overcoats, got away with a £62,500 payroll theft at London Airport.

**Thursday 29**    "**More Children in Council Care.**" The number of children in care in England and Wales at March this year, reached 63,648 at a cost of £20m a year.

**Friday 30**    "**Wealthy Earl's Son Wins the Princess.**" It was announced last night that company director Angus Ogilvy is to marry Princess Alexandra the Queen's cousin and granddaughter of George V. The wedding ceremony will be attended by all the members of the royal family and broadcast worldwide on television.

**Sat 1st Dec**    "**Jellied Eels Up a Tanner.**" Increased demand from Europe for British eels has put the price of east Londoner's favourite food up by a tanner, (6d) from 2 shillings (10p) a bowl to 2s 6d (12.5p).

**Sunday 2**    "**Call to Increase the Age of Criminal Responsibility.**" Three Labour Peers are calling for the minimum age to be raised from eight to twelve years.

## HERE IN BRITAIN

### "The Tr-r-r-rain Now St-t-t-tanding On ..."

If you cannot make out what the train announcer is saying at Charing Cross station it is because their teeth are chattering with the cold. The 30ft high crows' nest from which the departure times are broadcast has no heating and the announcers have sent a complaint to Brr-r-itish Railways.

They say that in winter they sit with their legs wrapped in newspaper and tucked into a cardboard box to keep warm, but the cold still seeps up through the floorboards from a public convenience below and, they say, "It's like sitting in a fridge."

## AROUND THE WORLD

### "Non-Stop TV Girl Raises A Million."

The greatest charity show in history was held this week in Holland when Mies Bouwman, their leading TV announcer, compered 23 hours of non-stop variety from 400 big names on radio and television.

Chain smoking and drinking milk to keep going, Mies pleaded with the public to "give" and the fantastic response at the end of the show, was £1.2m – but the giving didn't end there, people continued to hand over cash, cars, jewellery – even cattle – to help build a village for handicapped people.

# Concord Over Concorde

Britain and France this week signed an agreement for the joint development of the world's first supersonic airliner, a Mach 2.2 transport which should be flying by 1966 and ready for airline service by 1970. The total cost will be about £160m. This slim, delta-winged aircraft will cut the Atlantic crossing time from seven and a half hours to about three hours and the London to Sydney flying time from 27 hours to 13 hours.

Called the Concord (Concorde in France), the supersonic transport will cruise at 55,000ft to 60,000ft, will be designed to operate from ordinary runways at London Airport, with a landing speed of some 145 knots, similar to that of present large jet types. A retractable visor will be raised in supersonic flight to reduce aerodynamic drag, the pilot flying on instruments and with the aid of a periscope. The visor will be lowered in subsonic flight to provide normal vision for the pilot.

The British Aircraft Corporation and the French Sud Aviation company will carry out together the work on the air- frame, making two versions of the aircraft, one long-range and the other medium-range. Both variants will be powered by four civil versions of the Olympus 593 turbo- jet engine which is to be employed in the RAF's TSR 2 supersonic strike and reconnaissance aircraft. Bristol Siddeley and the French SNECMA company will develop the civil engine jointly and it is thought that damage resulting from the sonic boom would be negligible. BAC said that on the ground, the noise produced by the airliner was expected to be little more than that from present subsonic jets.

France and Britain will share the costs, the work and the proceeds of sales.

# DEC 3RD - DEC 9TH 1962

## IN THE NEWS

**Monday 3**     **"Tanker Terminal for Felixstowe."** A terminal is to be built at the mouth of the River Orwell to compete for the growing import business of cut-price Continental petrol.

**Tuesday 4**     **"Fire Destroys Vulcan Testing Secret Engine."** Development work on the new Concord supersonic airplane engine may be delayed by several months after fire swept through the factory.

**Wednesday 5**     **"Nightmare Britain – Smog, Fog, Ice!"** Visibility nil. That was the grim report from much of freezing, fog-bound Britain last night and in London, the dense fog was officially smog as it combined smoke from millions of coal fires.

**Thursday 6**     **"Longest Day of the Spurs Fans."** Spurs supporters braved a ten-hour train journey through ice, fog, muddle and delay to get to the European Cup game against Rangers in Glasgow, only to find the match postponed because of fog.

**Friday 7**     **"Chancellor Says No."** Reginald Maudling dashed hopes for extra help for the unemployed by rejecting appeals for a pre-Christmas boost to unemployment pay – or any other welfare benefits.

**Saturday 8**     **"Cost of the Big Smog."** During the last four days, 116 people died, 947 were taken to hospital, cost to London Transport was £150,000 in lost fares and the AA's bills for breakdowns, rose by £50,000. MPs are asking why we have this terrible smog every year in London and that burning smoky coal should be banned.

**Sunday 9**     **"Rebels Seize Shell Company Installations."** British troops are helping hunt the Secret Army leaders waging war against the British protected State of Brunei in Borneo.

## HERE IN BRITAIN

### "Smog Emergency In London"

Smog is a concentration of smoke particles and other substances such as sulphur dioxide, combined with fog. Sulphur dioxide is produced by petrol engines, coal and even some smokeless fuel.

If the conditions are as they were this week, low temperature, high pressure and lack of wind, when the fog forms, it settles at a low level and there is no wind to blow it away. The low temperatures reduce rising warm air and all this means fumes and particles produced by cars and most forms of burning are trapped in the fog forming a health threatening 'pea souper'.

## AROUND THE WORLD

### "A Man With 'No Land Of His Own Fathers' Just Loves Saying Wales"

Joacquim Reimunto comes from Uruguay and has lost his identity card and with it any interest Uruguay might have taken in him. He has sailed 10,000 miles looking for a country prepared to 'adopt' him and landed this week in a country he never knew existed – Wales. He is awaiting to hear if he will be allowed to stay.

Now he says, 'Wales' is the loveliest word he has ever heard – he keeps repeating it with tender intonation – for it has given him a three-month respite from his restless pilgrimage as a stateless person.

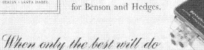

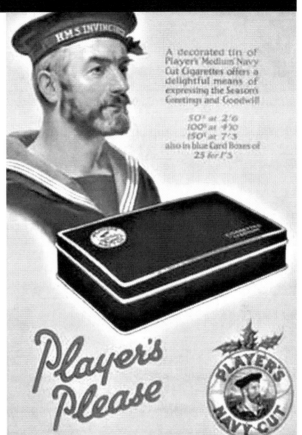

There was a drop of 2,100 million (to 91,300 million) in the number of plain cigarettes sold in the UK last year, compared with the 1960 figure but sales of tipped cigarettes rose by 4,600 million to a total of 22,100 million. Rolling tobacco sales rose but cigar sales remained the same at 315 million.

During 1961 the consumption of manufactured cigarettes for an adult male dropped from 4,030 to 4,010 but at the same time the figure for women smokers rose from 1,620 to 1,680. The figures show that the greatest percentage of smokers, both men and women, are in the 35-49 year age group.

The men smoking an average of 91 cigarettes a week, and the women 46. Smokers aged 25-34 years inhale the most. 30% of men started to smoke while still under 16 years old and by the age of 19, 78%of the men were smoking. Only 10% of women began before they were 16.

1.8 million men smoked tipped cigarettes and 9 million smoked plain cigarettes, plain cigarettes dropping by 25% in the last five years, losing out as people move to tipped varieties . Pipe smokers also dropped in number during the three years, from 3.1 million to 2.6 million. Marital status also played its part and the figures show that while more unmarried men than married men smoked cigarettes, more married women than unmarried women smoked. But married pipe smokers were in the majority over bachelors.

The heaviest smoker last year, on the social scale, was the upper middle class man, who smoked an average 146 cigarettes a week while the upper middle class woman smoked an average of 75 cigarettes. The heaviest smoker among the women was the skilled working class, with an average of 80 cigarettes a week.

## IN THE NEWS

**Monday 10**    "**Gurkhas Ambushed.**" British army Gurkha soldiers were flown into Brunei to defend the Sultan against rebels who threatened the Shell oilfields.

**Tuesday 11**    "**Storm Over Squalid BAOR Homes.**" A British Army of the Rhine housing muddle has forced families into squalid lodgings as they wait for their married quarters. The accommodation was damp with bedroom walls covered in mould and the heating was inadequate.

**Wednesday 12**    "**Battle of Dartmoor.**" Thirty of Dartmoor's toughest prisoners battled with prison officers in a jail workshop yesterday. Five officers were injured in the worst outbreak of violence at the Princetown jail since the 1932 mutiny.

**Thursday 13**    "**Brunei Prisoners' Ordeal and the Nurse's Heroism.**" Courageous hostage, nurse Jean Scott, refused to take a rebel leader to hospital until all women and children hostages were released.

**Friday 14**    "**Skybolt: US tells Britain to Go It Alone.**" The US made a final offer before cancelling the Skybolt ballistic missile project. You can take it over if you pay for it.

**Saturday 15**    "**Mariner 2 Makes It.**" Bang on target, bang on time, the US space-ship passed within 21,000 miles of Venus precisely as planned when it was launched in August.

**Sunday 16**    "**Berlin Bomb Tears Gap in the Wall.**" A West German policeman said, "It's the best job so far!" meaning it was the biggest of all the attempts to blow holes in the wall between east and west Berlin since it was built.

### HERE IN BRITAIN
**"Bookworm With A Conscience."**

An avid reader has openly returned 299 books to Norwich library - all taken out illegally by him over the past 16 years. The collection, a wide range of fiction and non-fiction, had been listed as missing by library staff, the earliest in 1946.

During removal operations to their new library, just completed, all overdue books could be returned, "with no questions asked". "When he drove up to the new library with all these books in a van," said the City librarian, "my staff were flabbergasted."

We have assured him that as far as we are concerned the matter is closed. In fact, we are grateful to him".

### AROUND THE WORLD
**"White Funeral For A Former Queen."**

Princess Wilhelmina, who was for 50 years, Queen of the Netherlands, was laid to rest in the family vaults at Delft this week.

Eight horses draped in white drew a white coach bearing her body and a second white coach had a profusion of white flowers.

In her book *'Lonely but Not Alone'*, Princess Wilhelmina wrote, "Long before he died, my husband and I had discussed the meaning of death and the eternal life that follows it. Death is the beginning of life and therefore we had promised that we would both have white funerals".

# US-UK MISSILE ABANDONED

This week the US Skybolt air-launched ballistic missile project was cancelled. The basic concept of Skybolt was to allow US strategic bombers to launch their weapons from well outside the range of Soviet defences. The UK joined the Skybolt programme intending to use it on our V Bomber force and the UK had decided to base our entire deterrent force on the missile.

From a the purely military point of view the missile no longer has any real place in the US strategic plan. Quite apart from the technical failure of the missiles which have been tested, there are serious doubts about the value of the whole concept of firing ballistic missiles from aircraft. Basically there are almost insuperable problems of accurate aiming from a platform which is moving very quickly and which may also be unstable.

Declarations attributed to the Ministry of Defence that the cancellation of the Skybolt programme might mean a radical reappraisal of British defence policy have caused no dismay among Americans even though it may drive Britain into a close association with France in the development of ballistic missiles. Britain has a vast fund of technical knowledge enabling the French to develop an effective nuclear striking force more quickly and more cheaply than on their own.

French observers are already enthusiastically referring to Skybolt as the "pomme de discorde" between the United States and Britain and see this as an opportunity to boost their own military equipment industry and status.

# DEC 17TH - DEC 23RD 1962

## IN THE NEWS

**Monday 17**  "Here Comes Santa". Forty youngsters from the displaced persons camps of central Europe, now living at the Pestalozzi Village in Sussex, were thrilled when Santa dropped in by helicopter.

**Tuesday 18**  "Sea of Treacle Stops Traffic." Dozens of cars were stuck last night on a road near Gloucester, which was flooded with treacle from an overturned tanker. Local police warned drivers to avoid the area as the situation was 'sticky'.

**Wednesday 19**  "The All-Clear for Pay TV Try Out." The Government gave the Independent Television Authority the go ahead to start trials on a Pay-As-You-View television service.

**Thursday 20**  "Sunshine Lights Up Shops Boom." The bad weather, ice and smog of the last week delayed Christmas shopping until yesterday when the sunshine brought out droves of shoppers.

**Friday 21**  "It's Polaris or Nothing". President Kennedy has offered Mr Macmillan Polaris as Britain's independent nuclear deterrent instead of Skybolt, on a take it or leave it basis.

**Saturday 22**  "NATO Will Control Britain's Polaris Subs." Britain and America are to pool nuclear forces for the defence of the West, and they have asked France to do the same.

**Sunday 23**  "1s 6d a lb! Turkeys cheaper than stewing steak." Late last night, London's Smithfield Meat market was selling large, frozen, oven-ready turkeys 'for a song' and today, will auction off the rest of their stock. (*Ed Note - 1s 6d a lb is 15p a kilo*)

## HERE IN BRITAIN

**"Demob Hungry Candidates".**

Hundreds of Servicemen seeking a free discharge by applying to fight the parliamentary by-election in Rotherham, Yorkshire, are finding it won't be quite that easy!

They learned by letter this week that no matter where they are stationed, they must arrange for a Rotherham voter to collect the by-election nomination paper.

Plus, each must find ten more Rotherham citizens, a proposer, a seconder and eight others to sign his nomination paper and, each man may well have to put down £150 in cash. All of which should lead to the "big fall-out."

## AROUND THE WORLD

**"Mona Lisa Arrives In The US."**

The 'Mona Lisa' arrived safely in the United States this week after its journey across the Atlantic in the liner 'France'.

As the ship docked in New York at dawn on Thursday, the French guards who have been watching over the painting since it left Paris were joined by United States secret service men who have been ordered to guard it 24 hours a day for as long as it remains in the USA.

After being shown at the National Gallery in Washington for three weeks it will return to New York for display at the Metropolitan Museum.

# CANNED MUSIC ON THE PROM

Whilst the biting rain and wind made pedestrians shiver behind turned-up collars, the soft, warm tones of 'La vie en rose' was being directed from almost every lamp post on the Promenade in Blackpool this week. Hoping to maintain its reputation of being first in the field, Blackpool is experimenting with broadcast "canned" music in the town centre at the suggestion of councillor who wants Blackpool to *"get back to being a town of song and melody"*.

*"Military band concerts and the like would cost too much and only reach a handful of people"*, the councillor said. *"What we wanted was subdued music which, although people don't notice it, wipes out of their minds, thoughts of strikes or atom bombs or whatever it is that makes them look so sombre as they walk about"*. When asked if the scheme would interfere with the individual's freedom to choose whether he wants to hear music wherever he goes, he said, *"I don't think you can compare this with youngsters walking round with transistor radios blaring rock 'n' roll and that rumbustious 'trad' jazz,"* he replied, *"we are thinking of light music, Franz Lehar or Palm Court stuff, you know. I think the people who would complain about that are real Scrooges"*.

Many people in the streets welcomed the council's enterprise. *"Lots of folk thought the illuminations were a silly idea, but look at the trade they bring in now"*, a shopkeeper said. Many shoppers did not notice the carols and songs until the muted tones filling the two streets was brought to their attention. *"Ah well"*, sighed one middle-aged gentleman, struggling with his wife's Christmas parcels as *"God rest ye merry, gentlemen"*, floated from above, *"a bit of peace and quiet's getting rarer and rarer. I dare say we shall have to soon pay for it if we're not careful."*

# DEC 24TH - DEC 31ST 1962

## IN THE NEWS

**Monday 24** — "**Cuba Releases the Last Prisoners.**" Over a thousand American troops held since 'The Bay of Pigs' invasion, were released in exchange for food worth $53million.

**Tuesday 25** — "**Christmas On Ice in Brr-itain.**" Cold and crisp, that's the outlook for a sparkling Christmas. Frosty and dry over most of the country.

**Wednesday 26** — "**Boxing Day Snow Storm Rail Disaster.**" 17 people were killed and 50 injured when the Glasgow to London express ploughed into the back of another main-line train at Crewe. The impact was severe and caused the train to be pushed forward some 140 ft. (45m).

**Thursday 27** — "**Melody Maker Votes Frank Ifield, The Best of the Year.**" "I Remember You" is voted the best single disc of 1962, selling 1million copies.

**Friday 28** — "**Doctors Fight for Cash.**" Shortage of money may force a shutdown of the "miracle" research department at Hammersmith hospital. World famous for achievements in heart and kidney surgery and separating Siamese Twins.

**Saturday 29** — "**Fog … Now We've Got the Lot.**" Fog plus the recent ice and snow brought wide-spread dangers on the roads with no let-up of the Big Freeze in sight.

**Sunday 30** — "**Graham Hill World Champion Racing Driver.**" Hill won the South African Grand Prix yesterday in an all-British BRM to take the title.

**Monday 31** — "**Mr Billy Butlin Saves Hospital**". The holiday camp millionaire has given Hammersmith Hospital £30,000 for continued research into kidney graft surgery.

## HERE IN BRITAIN

### "Hot Water Bottle Ban Must Go."

A plea to lift a ban on hot water bottle for cold toed hospital patients is made this week. "If the pattern of the patient's day is to resemble as closely as possible his life at home, then a hot water bottle in a cold bed seems essential," declares an editorial in the Nursing Times.

Hospitals claim the ban made by hospital administrators is the fear of court actions following hot water bottle burns, "But thousands, if not millions of people, fill bottles in their own homes without fearful consequences."

## AROUND THE WORLD

### "Somerset Maugham Adopts A Son."

The 88 year-old novelist and playwright, has adopted his 60-year-old private secretary, Mr Alan Searle, as his son. The writer wants to cancel the bequest of his £360,000 villa at Cap Ferrat on the French Riviera, to his daughter and has summoned her to appear in a Nice court for the annulment of the bequest.

He is also taking legal action in England to cancel a £580,000 trust fund set up for his daughter's two children and he intends to make over his fortune, estimated at £1m, to Mr Searle who has been his secretary for 33 years.

# BUS BURSTS INTO BERLIN

*East Germans Look Over The Berlin Wall Into The West*

Two East German families including four children, escaped over Christmas to West Berlin in a bus covered with home-made armour plating. The bus broke through three border barriers under a hail of gunfire from Communist guards. Eight bullets pierced the side, but missed the refugees huddling on the floor. The only injury was caused by a glass splinter that cut the driver's thumb. The leader of the group, was the bus owner, Hans Weidner, a war cripple who walks with crutches and is an expert motor mechanic.

He had planned the escape for six months from his home town near the Polish border, 150 miles from Berlin. With his younger driver, Jurgen Wagner, he built a snow plough on the front of the bus and 4 inch spikes into the hubs of the front wheels to cut through barbed wire. To protect the tyres they put metal plates around the wheels. Steel plates were placed along the sides of the bus and in case police wondered what they were doing near Berlin, the two men hung signs reading "repair bus" on the front and rear.

On Christmas Eve they set out with their wives and children – three girls, aged one, three and thirteen and a boy of ten. Mr Weidner said, "We hoped to break through the same day but halfway to Berlin, we broke down. We left the women and children in different wayside inns and Jurgen and I went back home for spare parts." Where, to avoid suspicion, he spent part of Christmas at a local bar … pretending to be drunk. Then through most of Christmas night, the two men worked in sub-zero temperatures to get the bus going.

They reached Berlin on Boxing Day, circled the city, then at dawn they approached the East German control point. Jurgen, the driver, gave two friendly honks and flashed his headlights to make the guards think it was an ordinary lorry. They drove at regulation speed of 15mph. Then, as they reached the post, he accelerated. It was a moment before the guards realised what was happening and opened fire. At the next barrier, the bus headlights were shot out, but the bus roared on, past a third blockade, across a mile of 'no man's land' and into the American sector of Berlin.

# 1962 Calendar

## January

| S | M | T | W | T | F | S |
|---|---|---|---|---|---|---|
|   | 1 | 2 | 3 | 4 | 5 | 6 |
| 7 | 8 | 9 | 10 | 11 | 12 | 13 |
| 14 | 15 | 16 | 17 | 18 | 19 | 20 |
| 21 | 22 | 23 | 24 | 25 | 26 | 27 |
| 28 | 29 | 30 | 31 |   |   |   |

## February

| S | M | T | W | T | F | S |
|---|---|---|---|---|---|---|
|   |   |   |   | 1 | 2 | 3 |
| 4 | 5 | 6 | 7 | 8 | 9 | 10 |
| 11 | 12 | 13 | 14 | 15 | 16 | 17 |
| 18 | 19 | 20 | 21 | 22 | 23 | 24 |
| 25 | 26 | 27 | 28 |   |   |   |

## March

| S | M | T | W | T | F | S |
|---|---|---|---|---|---|---|
|   |   |   |   | 1 | 2 | 3 |
| 4 | 5 | 6 | 7 | 8 | 9 | 10 |
| 11 | 12 | 13 | 14 | 15 | 16 | 17 |
| 18 | 19 | 20 | 21 | 22 | 23 | 24 |
| 25 | 26 | 27 | 28 | 29 | 30 | 31 |

## April

| S | M | T | W | T | F | S |
|---|---|---|---|---|---|---|
| 1 | 2 | 3 | 4 | 5 | 6 | 7 |
| 8 | 9 | 10 | 11 | 12 | 13 | 14 |
| 15 | 16 | 17 | 18 | 19 | 20 | 21 |
| 22 | 23 | 24 | 25 | 26 | 27 | 28 |
| 29 | 30 |   |   |   |   |   |

## May

| S | M | T | W | T | F | S |
|---|---|---|---|---|---|---|
|   |   | 1 | 2 | 3 | 4 | 5 |
| 6 | 7 | 8 | 9 | 10 | 11 | 12 |
| 13 | 14 | 15 | 16 | 17 | 18 | 19 |
| 20 | 21 | 22 | 23 | 24 | 25 | 26 |
| 27 | 28 | 29 | 30 | 31 |   |   |

## June

| S | M | T | W | T | F | S |
|---|---|---|---|---|---|---|
|   |   |   |   |   | 1 | 2 |
| 3 | 4 | 5 | 6 | 7 | 8 | 9 |
| 10 | 11 | 12 | 13 | 14 | 15 | 16 |
| 17 | 18 | 19 | 20 | 21 | 22 | 23 |
| 24 | 25 | 26 | 27 | 28 | 29 | 30 |

## July

| S | M | T | W | T | F | S |
|---|---|---|---|---|---|---|
| 1 | 2 | 3 | 4 | 5 | 6 | 7 |
| 8 | 9 | 10 | 11 | 12 | 13 | 14 |
| 15 | 16 | 17 | 18 | 19 | 20 | 21 |
| 22 | 23 | 24 | 25 | 26 | 27 | 28 |
| 29 | 30 | 31 |   |   |   |   |

## August

| S | M | T | W | T | F | S |
|---|---|---|---|---|---|---|
|   |   |   | 1 | 2 | 3 | 4 |
| 5 | 6 | 7 | 8 | 9 | 10 | 11 |
| 12 | 13 | 14 | 15 | 16 | 17 | 18 |
| 19 | 20 | 21 | 22 | 23 | 24 | 25 |
| 26 | 27 | 28 | 29 | 30 | 31 |   |

## September

| S | M | T | W | T | F | S |
|---|---|---|---|---|---|---|
|   |   |   |   |   |   | 1 |
| 2 | 3 | 4 | 5 | 6 | 7 | 8 |
| 9 | 10 | 11 | 12 | 13 | 14 | 15 |
| 16 | 17 | 18 | 19 | 20 | 21 | 22 |
| 23 | 24 | 25 | 26 | 27 | 28 | 29 |
| 30 |   |   |   |   |   |   |

## October

| S | M | T | W | T | F | S |
|---|---|---|---|---|---|---|
|   | 1 | 2 | 3 | 4 | 5 | 6 |
| 7 | 8 | 9 | 10 | 11 | 12 | 13 |
| 14 | 15 | 16 | 17 | 18 | 19 | 20 |
| 21 | 22 | 23 | 24 | 25 | 26 | 27 |
| 28 | 29 | 30 | 31 |   |   |   |

## November

| S | M | T | W | T | F | S |
|---|---|---|---|---|---|---|
|   |   |   |   | 1 | 2 | 3 |
| 4 | 5 | 6 | 7 | 8 | 9 | 10 |
| 11 | 12 | 13 | 14 | 15 | 16 | 17 |
| 18 | 19 | 20 | 21 | 22 | 23 | 24 |
| 25 | 26 | 27 | 28 | 29 | 30 |   |

## December

| S | M | T | W | T | F | S |
|---|---|---|---|---|---|---|
|   |   |   |   |   |   | 1 |
| 2 | 3 | 4 | 5 | 6 | 7 | 8 |
| 9 | 10 | 11 | 12 | 13 | 14 | 15 |
| 16 | 17 | 18 | 19 | 20 | 21 | 22 |
| 23 | 24 | 25 | 26 | 27 | 28 | 29 |
| 30 | 31 |   |   |   |   |   |

Printed in Poland
by Amazon Fulfillment
Poland Sp. z o.o., Wrocław
28 November 2022

7f7762c0-3df9-4571-929a-8d3672dc70a3R01